The Great Conspiracy - Part V

JOHN ALEXANDER LOGAN

New York 1886

TABLE OF CONTENTS

FREEDOM PROCLAIMED TO ALL

While mentally revolving the question of Emancipation—now, evidently "coming to a head,"—no inconsiderable portion of Mr. Lincoln's thoughts centered upon, and his perplexities grew out of, his assumption that the "physical difference" between the Black and White—the African and Caucasian races, precluded the idea of their living together in the one land as Free men and equals.

In his speeches during the great Lincoln-Douglas debate we have seen this idea frequently advanced, and so, in his later public utterances as President.

As in his appeal to the Congressional delegations from the Border-States on the 12th of July, 1862, he had held out to them the hope that "the Freed people will not be so reluctant to go" to his projected colony in South America, when their "numbers shall be large enough to be company and encouragement for one another," so, at a later date—on the 14th of August following—he appealed to the Colored Free men themselves to help him found a proposed Negro colony in New Granada, and thus aid in the solution of this part of the knotty problem, by the disenthrallment of the new race from its unhappy environments here.

The substance of the President's interesting address, at the White House, to the delegation of Colored men, for whom he had sent, was thus reported at the time:

"Having all been seated, the President, after a few preliminary observations, informed them that a sum of money had been appropriated by Congress, and placed at his disposition, for the purpose of aiding the colonization in some country of the people, or a portion of them, of African descent, thereby making it his duty, as it had for a long time been his inclination, to favor that cause; and why, he asked, should the people of your race be colonized, and where?

"Why should they leave this Country? This is perhaps the first question for proper consideration. You and we are different races. We have between us a broader difference than exists between almost any other two races. Whether it is right or wrong I need not discuss; but this physical difference is a great disadvantage to us both, as I think. Your race suffers very greatly, many of them by living among us, while ours suffers from your presence. In a word we suffer on each side. If this is admitted, it affords a reason, at least, why we should be separated. You here are Freemen, I suppose?

"A VOICE—Yes, Sir.

"THE PRESIDENT—Perhaps you have long been free, or all your lives. Your race are suffering, in my judgment, the greatest wrong inflicted on any people. But even when you cease to be Slaves, you are yet far removed from being placed on an equality with the White race. You are cut off from many of the advantages which the other race enjoys. The aspiration of men is to enjoy equality with the best when free; but on this broad continent not a single man of your race is made the equal of a single man of ours. Go where you are treated the best, and the ban is still upon you. I do not propose to discuss this, but to present it as a fact, with which we have to deal. I cannot alter it if I would. It is a fact about which we all think and feel alike, I and you. We look to our condition.

"Owing to the existence of the two races on this continent, I need not recount to you the effects upon White men, growing out of the institution of Slavery. I believe in its general evil effects on the White race. See our present condition—the Country engaged in War! our white men cutting one another's throats—none knowing how far it will extend—and then consider what we know to be the truth. But for your race among us there could not be War, although many men engaged on either side do not care for you one way or the other. Nevertheless, I repeat, without the institution of Slavery, and the Colored race as a basis, the War could not have an existence. It is better for us both, therefore, to be separated.

"I know that there are Free men among you who, even if they could better their condition, are not as much inclined to go out of the Country as those who, being Slaves, could obtain their Freedom on this condition. I suppose one of the principal difficulties in the way of colonization is that the free colored man cannot see that his comfort would be advanced by it. You may believe that you can live in Washington, or elsewhere in the United States, the remainder of your life; perhaps more so than you can in any foreign country, and hence you may come to the conclusion that you have nothing to do with the idea of going to a foreign country.

"This is, (I speak in no unkind sense) an extremely selfish view of the case. But you ought to do something to help those who are not so fortunate as yourselves. There is an unwillingness on the part of our People, harsh as it may be, for you free Colored people to remain with us. Now if you could give a start to the White people you would open a wide door for many to be made free. If we deal with those who are not free at the beginning, and whose intellects are clouded by Slavery, we have very poor material to start with.

"If intelligent Colored men, such as are before me, could move in this matter, much might be accomplished. It is exceedingly important that we have men at the beginning capable of thinking as White men, and not those who have been systematically oppressed. There is much to encourage you.

"For the sake of your race you should sacrifice something of your present comfort for the purpose of being as grand in that respect as the White people. It is a cheering thought throughout life, that something can be done to ameliorate the condition of those who have been subject to the hard usages of the World. It is difficult to make a man miserable while he feels he is worthy of himself and claims kindred to the great God who made him.

"In the American Revolutionary War, sacrifices were made by men engaged in it, but they were cheered by the future. General Washington himself endured greater physical hardships than if he had remained a British subject, yet he was a happy man, because he was engaged in benefiting his race, in doing something for the children of his neighbors, having none of his own.

"The Colony of Liberia has been in existence a long time. In a certain sense it is a success. The old President of Liberia, Roberts, has just been with me the first time I ever saw him. He says they have, within the bounds of that Colony, between three and four hundred thousand people, or more than in some of our old States, such as Rhode Island, or Delaware, or in some of our newer States, and less than in some of our larger ones. They are not all American colonists or their descendants. Something less than 12,000 have been sent thither from this Country. Many of the original settlers have died, yet, like people elsewhere, their offspring outnumber those deceased.

"The question is, if the Colored people are persuaded to go anywhere, why not there? One reason for unwillingness to do so is that some of you would rather remain within reach of the country of your nativity. I do not know how much attachment you may have toward our race. It does not strike me that you have the greatest reason to love them. But still you are attached to them at all events.

"The place I am thinking about having for a colony, is in Central America. It is nearer to us than Liberia—not much more than one-fourth as far as Liberia, and within seven days' run by steamers. Unlike Liberia, it is a great line of travel—it is a highway. The country is a very excellent one for any people, and with great natural resources and advantages, and especially because of the similarity of climate with your native soil, thus being suited

7

to your physical condition.

"The particular place I have in view, is to be a great highway from the Atlantic or Caribbean Sea to the Pacific Ocean, and this particular place has all the advantages for a colony. On both sides there are harbors among the finest in the World. Again, there is evidence of very rich coal mines. A certain amount of coal is valuable in any country. Why I attach so much importance to coal is, it will afford an opportunity to the inhabitants for immediate employment till they get ready to settle permanently in their homes.

"If you take colonists where there is no good landing, there is a bad show; and so, where there is nothing to cultivate, and of which to make a farm. But if something is started so that you can get your daily bread as soon as you reach there, it is a great advantage. Coal land is the best thing I know of, with which to commence an enterprise.

"To return—you have been talked to upon this subject, and told that a speculation is intended by gentlemen who have an interest in the country, including the coal mines. We have been mistaken all our lives if we do not know Whites, as well as Blacks, look to their self-interest. Unless among those deficient of intellect, everybody you trade with makes something. You meet with these things here and everywhere. If such persons have what will be an advantage to them, the question is, whether it cannot be made of advantage to you?

"You are intelligent, and know that success does not as much depend on external help, as on self-reliance. Much, therefore, depends upon yourselves. As to the coal mines, I think I see the means available for your self-reliance. I shall, if I get a sufficient number of you engaged, have provision made that you shall not be wronged. If you will engage in the enterprise, I will spend some of the money intrusted to me. I am not sure you will succeed. The Government may lose the money, but we cannot succeed unless we try; but we think, with care, we can succeed.

"The political affairs in Central America are not in quite as satisfactory condition as I wish. There are contending factions in that quarter; but it is true, all the factions are agreed alike on the subject of colonization, and want it; and are more generous than we are here. To your Colored race they have no objection. Besides, I would endeavor to have you made equals, and have the best assurance that you should be the equals of the best.

"The practical thing I want to ascertain is, whether I can get a number of able-bodied men, with their wives and children, who are willing to go, when I present evidence of encouragement and protection. Could I get a hundred tolerably intelligent men, with their wives and children, and able to 'cut their own fodder' so to speak? Can I have fifty? If I could find twenty-five able-bodied men, with a mixture of women and children—good things in the family relation, I think I could make a successful commencement.

"I want you to let me know whether this can be done or not. This is the practical part of my wish to see you. These are subjects of very great importance—worthy of a month's study, of a speech delivered in an hour. I ask you, then, to consider seriously, not as pertaining to yourselves merely, nor for your race, and ours, for the present time, but as one of the things, if successfully managed, for the good of mankind—not confined to the present generation, but as:

'From age to age descends the lay
To millions yet to be,
Till far its echoes roll away
Into eternity.'"

President Lincoln's well-meant colored colonization project, however, fell through, owing partly to opposition to it in Central America, and partly to the very natural and deeply-rooted disinclination of the Colored free men to leave the land of their birth.

Meanwhile, limited Military Emancipation of Slaves was announced and regulated, on the 22d July, 1862, by the following Executive Instructions, which were issued from the War Department by order of the President— the issue of which was assigned by Jefferson Davis as one reason for his Order of August 1, 1862, directing "that the commissioned officers of Pope's and Steinwehr's commands be not entitled, when captured, to be treated as soldiers and entitled to the benefit of the cartel of exchange:"

"WAR DEPARTMENT,

"WASHINGTON, D.C., July 22, 1862.

"First. Ordered that Military Commanders within the States of Virginia, North Carolina, Georgia, Florida, Alabama, Mississippi, Louisiana, Texas, and Arkansas, in an orderly manner seize and use any property, real or personal, which may be necessary or convenient for their several commands, for supplies, or for other Military purposes; and that while property may be destroyed for proper Military objects, none shall be destroyed in wantonness or malice.

"Second. That Military and Naval Commanders shall employ as laborers, within and from said States, so many Persons of African descent as can be advantageously used for Military or Naval purposes, giving them reasonable wages for their labor.

"Third. That, as to both property, and Persons of African descent, accounts shall be kept sufficiently accurate and in detail to show quantities and amounts, and from whom both property and such Persons shall have come, as a basis upon which compensation can be made in proper cases; and the several departments of this Government shall attend to and perform their appropriate parts towards the execution of these orders.

"By Order of the President:

"EDWIN M. STANTON,

"Secretary of War."

On the 9th of August, 1862, Major General McClellan promulgated the Executive Order of July 22, 1862, from his Headquarters at Harrison's Landing, Va., with certain directions of his own, among which were the following:

"Inhabitants, especially women and children, remaining peaceably at their homes, must not be molested; and wherever commanding officers find families peculiarly exposed in their persons or property to marauding from this Army, they will, as heretofore, so far as they can do with safety and without detriment to the service, post guards for their protection.

"In protecting private property, no reference is intended to Persons held to service or labor by reason of African Descent. Such Persons will be regarded by this Army, as they heretofore have been, as occupying simply a peculiar legal status under State laws, which condition the Military authorities of the United States are not required to regard at all in districts where Military operations are made necessary by the rebellious action of the State governments.

"Persons subject to suspicion of hostile purposes, residing or being near our Forces, will be, as heretofore, subject to arrest and detention, until the cause or necessity is removed. All such arrested parties will be sent, as usual, to the Provost-Marshal General, with a statement of the facts in each case.

"The General Commanding takes this occasion to remind the officers and soldiers of this Army that we are engaged in supporting the Constitution and the Laws of the United States and suppressing Rebellion against their authority; that we are not engaged in a War of rapine, revenge, or subjugation; that this is not a contest against populations, but against armed forces and political organizations; that it is a struggle carried on with the United States, and should be conducted by us upon the highest principles known to Christian civilization.

"Since this Army commenced active operations, Persons of African descent, including those held to service or labor under State laws, have always been received, protected, and employed as laborers at wages. Hereafter it shall be the duty of the Provost-Marshal General to cause lists to be made of all persons of African descent employed in this Army as laborers for Military purposes—such lists being made sufficiently accurate and in detail to show from whom such persons shall have come.

"Persons so subject and so employed have always understood that after being received into the Military service of the United States, in any capacity, they could never be reclaimed by their former holders. Except upon such understanding on their part, the order of the President, as to this class of Persons, would be inoperative. The General Commanding therefore feels authorized to declare to all such employees, that they will receive permanent Military protection against any compulsory return to a condition of servitude."

Public opinion was now rapidly advancing, under the pressure of Military necessity, and the energetic efforts of the immediate Emancipationists, to a belief that Emancipation by Presidential Proclamation would be wise and efficacious as an instrumentality toward subduing the Rebellion; that it must come, sooner or later—and the sooner, the better.

Indeed, great fault was found, by some of these, with what they characterized as President Lincoln's "obstinate slowness" to come up to their advanced ideas on the subject. He was even accused of failing to execute existing laws touching confiscation of Slaves of Rebels coming within the lines of the Union Armies. On the 19th of August, 1862, a letter was addressed to him by Horace Greeley which concluded thus:

"On the face of this wide Earth, Mr. President, there is not one disinterested, determined, intelligent champion of the Union Cause who does not feel that all attempts to put down the Rebellion, and at the same time uphold its inciting cause, are preposterous and futile—that the Rebellion, if crushed out to-morrow, would be renewed within a year if Slavery were left in full vigor—that Army officers, who remain to this day devoted to Slavery, can at best be but half-way loyal to the Union—and that every hour of deference to Slavery is an hour of added and deepened peril to the Union.

"I appeal to the testimony of your embassadors in Europe. It is freely at your service, not mine. Ask them to tell you candidly whether the seeming subserviency of your policy to the Slaveholding, Slavery-upholding interest, is not the perplexity, the despair, of Statesmen of all parties; and be admonished by the general answer.

"I close, as I began, with the statement that what an immense majority of the loyal millions of your countrymen require of you, is a frank, declared, unqualified, ungrudging execution of the Laws of the Land, more especially of the Confiscation Act. That Act gives Freedom to the Slaves of Rebels coming within our lines, or whom those lines may at any time inclose. We ask you to render it due obedience by publicly requiring all your subordinates to recognize and obey it.

"The Rebels are everywhere using the late Anti-Negro riots in the North — as they have long used your officers' treatment of Negroes in the South—to convince the Slaves that they have nothing to hope from a Union success—that we mean in that case to sell them into a bitter Bondage to defray the cost of the War.

"Let them impress this as a truth on the great mass of their ignorant and credulous Bondmen, and the Union will never be restored—never. We can not conquer ten millions of people united in solid phalanx against us, powerfully aided by Northern sympathizers and European allies.

"We must have scouts, guides, spies, cooks, teamsters, diggers, and choppers, from the Blacks of the South—whether we allow them to fight for us or not—or we shall be baffled and repelled.

"As one of the Millions who would gladly have avoided this struggle, at any sacrifice but that of principle and honor, but who now feel that the triumph of the Union is indispensable not only to the existence of our Country, but to the well-being of mankind, I entreat you to render a hearty and unequivocal obedience to the Law of the Land.

"Yours,

"HORACE GREELEY."

To this letter, President Lincoln at once made the following memorable reply:

"EXECUTIVE MANSION,

"WASHINGTON, Friday, August 22, 1862.

"HON. HORACE GREELEY

"DEAR SIR:—I have just read yours of the 19th inst. addressed to myself through the New York Tribune.

"If there be in it any statements or assumptions of fact which I may know to be erroneous, I do not now and here controvert them.

"If there be any inferences which I may believe to be falsely drawn, I do not now and here argue against them.

"If there be perceptible in it an impatient and dictatorial tone, I waive it in deference to an old friend whose heart I have always supposed to be right.

"As to the policy I 'seem to be pursuing,' as you say, I have not meant to leave any one in doubt. I would save the Union. I would save it in the shortest way under the Constitution.

"The sooner the National authority can be restored, the nearer the Union will be—the Union as it was.

"If there be those who would not save the Union unless they could at the same time save Slavery, I do not agree with them.

"If there be those who would not save the Union unless they could at the same time destroy Slavery, I do not agree, with them.

"My paramount object is to save the Union and not either to save or destroy Slavery.

"If I could save the Union without freeing any Slave, I would do it—and if I could save it by freeing all the Slaves, I would do it—and if I could save it by freeing some and leaving others alone, I would also do that.

"What I do about Slavery and the Colored race, I do because I believe it helps to save the Union, and what I forbear, I forbear because I do not believe it would help to save the Union.

"I shall do less whenever I shall believe what I am doing hurts the cause, and shall do more whenever I believe doing more will help the cause.

"I shall try to correct errors when shown to be errors, and I shall adopt new views so fast as they shall appear to be true views.

"I have here stated my purpose according to my view of official duty, and I intend no modification of my oft-expressed personal wish that all men everywhere could be free.

"Yours,

"A. LINCOLN."

On the 13th of September, 1862, a deputation from all the religious denominations of Chicago presented to President Lincoln a memorial for the immediate issue of a Proclamation of Emancipation, to which, and the Chairman's remarks, he thus replied:

"The subject presented in the Memorial is one upon which I have thought much for weeks past, and I may even say, for months. I am approached with the most opposite opinions, and advice, and that by religious men, who are equally certain that they represent the Divine will. I am sure that either the one or the other class is mistaken in that belief, and perhaps, in some respects, both. I hope it will not be irreverent for me to say that if it is probable that God would reveal His will to others, on a point so connected with my duty, it might be supposed He would reveal it directly to me; for, unless I am more deceived in myself than I often am, it is my earnest desire to know the will of Providence in this matter. And if I can learn what it is, I will do it!

"These are not, however, the days of miracles, and I suppose it will be granted that I am not to expect a direct Revelation; I must study the plain physical aspects of the case, ascertain what is possible, and learn what appears to be wise and right!

"The subject is difficult, and good men do not agree. For instance, the other day, four gentlemen, of standing and intelligence, from New York, called, as a delegation, on business connected with the War; but, before leaving, two of them earnestly besought me to proclaim general Emancipation, upon which the other two at once attacked them.

"You know also that the last Session of Congress had a decided majority of Anti-Slavery men, yet they could not unite on this policy. And the same is true of the religious people; why the Rebel soldiers are praying with a great deal more earnestness, I fear, than our own troops, and expecting God to favor their side; for one of our soldiers, who had been taken prisoner, told Senator Wilson, a few days since, that he met nothing so discouraging as the evident sincerity of those he was among, in their prayers. But we will talk over the merits of the case.

"What good would a Proclamation of Emancipation from me do, especially as we are now situated? I do not want to issue a document that the whole World will see must necessarily be inoperative, like the Pope's Bull against the Comet! Would my word free the Slaves, when I cannot even enforce the Constitution in the Rebel States? Is there a single Court or Magistrate,

13

or individual that would be influenced by it there? And what reason is there to think it would have any greater effect upon the Slaves than the late law of Congress, which I approved and which offers protection and Freedom to the Slaves of Rebel masters who came within our lines? Yet I cannot learn that that law has caused a single Slave to come over to us.

"And suppose they could be induced by a Proclamation of Freedom from me to throw themselves upon us, what should we do with them? How can we feed and care for such a multitude? General Butler wrote me a few days since that he was issuing more rations to the Slaves who have rushed to him, than to all the White troops under his command. They eat, and that is all; though it is true General Butler is feeding the Whites also, by the thousand; for it nearly amounts to a famine there.

"If, now, the pressure of the War should call off our forces from New Orleans to defend some other point, what is to prevent the masters from reducing the Blacks to Slavery again; for I am told that whenever the Rebels take any Black prisoners, Free or Slave, they immediately auction them off! They did so with those they took from a boat that was aground in the Tennessee river a few days ago.

"And then I am very ungenerously attacked for it! For instance, when, after the late battles at and near Bull Run, an expedition went out from Washington, under a flag of truce, to bury the dead and bring in the wounded, and the Rebels seized the Blacks who went along to help, and sent them into Slavery, Horace Greeley said in his paper that the Government would probably do nothing about it. What could I do?

"Now, then, tell me, if you please, what possible result of good would follow the issuing of such a Proclamation as you desire? Understand, I raise no objections against it on legal or Constitutional grounds, for, as Commander-in-Chief of the Army and Navy, in time of War, I suppose I have a right to take any measure which may best subdue the Enemy, nor do I urge objections of a moral nature, in view of possible consequences of insurrection and massacre at the South. I view this matter as a practical War measure, to be decided on according to the advantages or disadvantages it may offer to the suppression of the Rebellion.

* * * * * * * * *

"I admit that Slavery is at the root of the Rebellion, or, at least, its sine qua non. The ambition of politicians may have instigated them to act, but they would have been impotent without Slavery as their instrument. I will also concede that Emancipation would help us in Europe, and convince them that we are incited by something more than ambition. I grant, further, that it would help somewhat at the North, though not so much, I fear, as you and those you represent imagine.

"Still, some additional strength would be added in that way to the War, and then, unquestionably, it would weaken the Rebels by drawing off their laborers, which is of great importance; but I am not so sure we could do much with the Blacks. If we were to arm them, I fear that in a few weeks the arms would be in the hands of the Rebels; and, indeed, thus far, we have not had arms enough to equip our White troops.

"I will mention another thing, though it meet only your scorn and contempt. There are 50,000 bayonets in the Union Army from the Border Slave States. It would be a serious matter if, in consequence of a Proclamation such as you desire, they should go over to the Rebels. I do not think they all would—not so many, indeed, as a year ago, or as six months ago—not so many to-day, as yesterday. Every day increases their Union feeling. They are also getting their pride enlisted, and want to beat the Rebels.

"Let me say one thing more: I think you should admit that we already have an important principle to rally and unite the People, in the fact that Constitutional Government is at stake. This is a fundamental idea going down about as deep as anything!

* * * * * * * * *

"Do not misunderstand me because I have mentioned these objections. They indicate the difficulties that have thus far prevented my action in some such way as you desire.

"I have not decided against a Proclamation of Liberty to the Slaves, but hold the matter under advisement. And I can assure you that the subject is on my mind, by day and night, more than any other. Whatever shall appear to be God's will I will do.

"I trust that in the freedom with which I have canvassed your views I have not in any respect injured your feelings."

On the 22d day of September, 1862, not only the Nation, but the whole World, was electrified by the publication—close upon the heels of the Union victory of Antietam—of the Proclamation of Emancipation—weighted with consequences so wide and far-reaching that even at this late day they cannot all be discerned. It was in these words:

"I, ABRAHAM LINCOLN, President of the United States of America, and Commander-in-Chief of the Army and Navy thereof, do hereby proclaim and declare that hereafter, as heretofore, the War will be prosecuted for the object of practically restoring the Constitutional relation between the United States and each of the States and the people thereof, in which States that relation is or may be suspended or disturbed.

"That it is my purpose, upon the next meeting of Congress, to again recommend the adoption of a practical measure tendering pecuniary aid to the free acceptance or rejection of all Slave States, so called, the people whereof may not then be in Rebellion against the United States, and which States may then have voluntarily adopted, or thereafter may voluntarily adopt, immediate or gradual abolishment of Slavery within their respective limits; and that the effort to colonize Persons of African descent with their consent upon this continent or elsewhere, with the previously obtained consent of the Governments existing there, will be continued.

"That on the first day of January, in the year of our Lord one thousand eight hundred and sixty-three, all Persons held as Slaves within any State or designated part of a State, the people whereof shall then be in Rebellion against the United States, shall be then, thenceforward, and forever Free; and the Executive Government of the United States, including the Military and Naval authority thereof, will recognize and maintain the Freedom of such persons, and will do no act or acts to repress such persons, or any of them, in any efforts they may make for their actual Freedom.

"That the Executive will, on the first day of January aforesaid, by Proclamation, designate the States and parts of States, if any, in which the people thereof respectively, shall then be in Rebellion against the United States; and the fact that any State, or the people thereof, shall on that day be, in good faith, represented in the Congress of the United States by members chosen thereto at elections wherein a majority of the qualified voters of such States shall have participated, shall, in the absence of strong countervailing testimony, be deemed conclusive evidence that such State, and the people thereof, are not in Rebellion against the United States.

"That attention is hereby called to an Act of Congress entitled 'An Act to make an additional Article of War,' approved March 31, 1862, and which Act is in the words and figures following:

"'Be it enacted by the Senate and House of Representatives of the United States of America in Congress assembled, That hereafter the following shall be promulgated as an additional Article of War, for the government of the Army of the United States, and shall be obeyed and observed as such.

"ARTICLE—All officers or persons in the Military or Naval service of the United States are prohibited from employing any of the forces under their respective commands for the purpose of returning Fugitives from service or labor who may have escaped from any persons to whom such service or labor is claimed to be due, and any officer who shall be found guilty by a court-martial of violating this article shall be dismissed from the service.

"'SECTION 2.—And be it further enacted, That this Act shall take effect from and after its passage.'

"Also to the ninth and tenth sections of an Act entitled 'An Act to suppress Insurrection, to punish Treason and Rebellion, to seize and confiscate property of Rebels, and for other purposes,' approved July 17, 1862, and which sections are in the words and figures following:

"'SEC. 9.—And be it further enacted, That all Slaves of persons who shall hereafter be engaged in Rebellion against the Government of the United States or who shall in any way give aid or comfort thereto, escaping from such persons and taking refuge within the lines of the Army; and all Slaves captured from such persons or deserted by them, and coming under the control of the Government of the United States; and all Slaves of such persons found on [or] being within any place occupied by Rebel forces and afterward occupied by the forces of the United States, shall be deemed captives of war, and shall be forever Free of their servitude, and not again held as Slaves.

"'SEC. 10.—And be it further enacted, That no Slave escaping into any State, Territory, or the District of Columbia, from any other State, shall be delivered up, or in any way impeded or hindered of his liberty, except for crime, or some offense against the laws, unless the person claiming said Fugitive shall first make oath that the person to whom the labor or service of such Fugitive is alleged to be due is his lawful owner, and has not borne arms against the United States in the present Rebellion, nor in any way given aid and comfort thereto; and no person engaged in the Military or Naval service of the United States shall, under any pretense whatever, assume to decide on the validity of the claim of any person to the service or labor of any other person, or surrender up any such Person to the claimant, on pain of being dismissed from the service."

"And I do hereby enjoin upon and order all persons engaged in the Military and Naval service of the United States to observe, obey, and enforce, within their respective spheres of service, the Act and sections above recited.

"And the Executive will in due time recommend that all citizens of the United States who shall have remained loyal thereto throughout the Rebellion shall (upon the restoration of the Constitutional relation between the United States and their respective States and people, if that relation shall have been suspended or disturbed) be compensated for all losses by acts of the United States, including the loss of Slaves.

"In witness whereof, I have hereunto set my hand, and caused the seal of the United States to be affixed.

"Done at the city of Washington this twenty-second day of September, in the year of our Lord one thousand eight hundred and sixty-two, and of the Independence of the United States the eighty-seventh.

"By the President:

"ABRAHAM LINCOLN.

"WILLIAM H. SEWARD, Secretary of State."

This Proclamation, promising Freedom to an Enslaved race, was hailed with acclamations everywhere save in the rebellious Southern-Slave States, and in the Border-Slave States.

At a meeting of Governors of Loyal States, held at Altoona, Pennsylvania, to take measures for the more active support of the Government, an Address was adopted, on the very day that the Proclamation was promulgated, which well expressed the general feeling prevailing throughout the Northern States, at this time. It was in these patriotic words:

"After nearly one year and a half spent in contest with an armed and gigantic Rebellion against the National Government of the United States, the duty and purpose of the Loyal States and people continue, and must always remain as they were at its origin—namely to restore and perpetuate the authority of this Government and the life of the Nation. No matter what consequences are involved in our fidelity, this work of restoring the Republic, preserving the institutions of democratic Liberty, and justifying the hopes and toils of our Fathers, shall not fail to be performed.

"And we pledge, without hesitation, to the President of the United States, the most loyal and cordial support, hereto as heretofore, in the exercise of the functions of his great office. We recognize in him the chief Executive magistrate of the Nation, the Commander-in-Chief of the Army and Navy of the United States, their responsible and constitutional head, whose rightful authority and power, as well as the Constitutional powers of Congress, must be rigorously and religiously guarded and preserved, as the condition on which alone our form of Government and the constitutional rights and liberties of the People themselves can be saved from the wreck of anarchy or from the gulf 'despotism.

"In submission to the laws which may have been or which may be duly enacted, and to the lawful orders of the President, cooperating always in our own spheres with the National Government, we mean to continue in the most rigorous exercise of all our lawful and proper powers, contending against Treason, Rebellion, and the public Enemies, and, whether in public life or in private station, supporting the arms of the Union, until its Cause shall conquer, until final victory shall perch upon its standard, or the Rebel foe will yield a dutiful, rightful, and unconditional submission. And, impressed with the conviction that an Army of reserve ought, until the War shall end, to be constantly kept on foot, to be raised, armed, equipped, and trained at home, and ready for emergencies, we respectfully ask the President to call such a force of volunteers for one year's service, of not less than one hundred thousand in the aggregate, the quota of each State to be raised after it shall have led its quota of the requisitions already made, both for volunteers and militia. We believe that this would be a Leasure of Military prudence, while it would greatly promote the Military education of the People.

"We hail with heartfelt gratitude and encouraged hope the Proclamation of the President, issued on the 22nd instant, declaring Emancipated from their bondage all Persons held to Service or Labor as Slaves in the Rebel States, whose Rebellion shall last until the first day of January next ensuing.

"The right of any person to retain authority to compel any portion of the subjects of the National Government to rebel against it, or to maintain its Enemies, implies in those who are allowed possession of such authority the right to rebel themselves; and therefore, the right to establish Martial Law or Military Government in a State or Territory in Rebellion implies the right and the duty of the Government to liberate the minds of all men living therein by appropriate Proclamations and assurances of protection, in order that all who are capable, intellectually and morally, of loyalty and obedience, may not be forced into Treason as the unwilling tools of rebellious Traitors.

"To have continued indefinitely the most efficient cause, support, and stay of the Rebellion, would have been, in our judgment, unjust to the Loyal people whose treasure and lives are made a willing sacrifice on the altar of patriotism—would have discriminated against the wife who is compelled to surrender her husband, against the parent who is to surrender his child, to the hardships of the camp and the perils of battle, in favor of Rebel masters permitted to retain their Slaves. It would have been a final decision alike against humanity, justice, the rights and dignity of the Government, and against sound and wise National policy.

"The decision of the President to strike at the root of the Rebellion will lend new vigor to efforts, and new life and hope to the hearts of the People. Cordially tendering to the President our respectful assurances of personal and official confidence, we trust and believe that the policy now inaugurated will be crowned with success, will give speedy and triumphant victories over our enemies, and secure to this Nation and this People the blessing and favor of Almighty God.

"We believe that the blood of the heroes who have already fallen, and those who may yet give their lives to their Country, will not have been shed in vain.

"The splendid valor of our soldiers, their patient endurance, their manly patriotism, and their devotion to duty, demand from us and from all their countrymen the homage of the sincerest gratitude and the pledge of our constant reinforcement and support. A just regard for these brave men, whom we have contributed to place in the field, and for the importance of the duties which may lawfully pertain to us hereafter, has called us into friendly conference.

"And now, presenting to our National Chief Magistrate this conclusion of our deliberations, we devote ourselves to our Country's service, and we will surround the President with our constant support, trusting that the fidelity and zeal of the Loyal States and People will always assure him that he will be constantly maintained in pursuing, with the utmost vigor, this War for the preservation of the National life and hope of humanity.

"A. G. CURTIN,
"JOHN A. ANDREW,
"RICHARD YATES,
"ISRAEL WASHBURNE, Jr.,
"EDWARD SOLOMON,
"SAMUEL J. KIRKWOOD,

"O. P. MORTON,—By D. G. ROSE, his Representative,
"WM. SPRAGUE,
"F. H. PEIRPOINT,
"DAVID TOD,
"N. S. BERRY, "AUSTIN BLAIR."

Some two months after the issue of his great Proclamation of Liberty, President Lincoln (in his Second Annual Message to Congress, December 1, 1862), took occasion again to refer to compensated Emancipation, and, indeed, to the entire matter of Slavery and Freedom, in most instructive and convincing manner, as follows:

"On the 22d day of September last, a Proclamation was issued by the Executive, a copy of which is herewith submitted.

"In accordance with the purpose in the second paragraph of that paper, I now respectfully recall your attention to what may be called 'compensated Emancipation.'

"A Nation may be said to consist of its territory, its people, and its laws. The territory is the only part which is of certain durability. 'One generation passeth away, and another generation cometh, but the Earth abideth forever.' It is of the first importance to duly consider and estimate this ever-enduring part.

"That portion of the Earth's surface which is owned and inhabited by the People of the United States, is well adapted to be the home of one National family; and it is not well adapted for two, or more. Its vast extent, and its variety of climate and productions, are of advantage, in this age, for one People, whatever they might have been in former ages. Steam, telegraphs, and intelligence, have brought these to be an advantageous combination for one united People.

"In the Inaugural Address I briefly pointed out the total inadequacy of Disunion, as a remedy for the differences between the people of the two Sections. I did so in language which I cannot improve, and which, therefore, I beg to repeat:

"'One Section of our Country believes Slavery is right, and ought to be extended, while the other believes it is wrong, and ought not to be extended. This is the only substantial dispute. The Fugitive Slave clause of the Constitution, and the law for the suppression of the foreign Slave Trade, are each as well enforced, perhaps, as any law can ever be in a community where the moral sense of the People imperfectly supports the law itself.

"The great body of the People abide by the dry legal obligation in both cases, and a few break over in each. This, I think, cannot be perfectly cured; and it would be worse in both cases after the separation of the Sections, than before. The foreign Slave Trade, now imperfectly suppressed, would be ultimately revived without restriction in one Section; while Fugitive

Slaves, now only partially surrendered, would not be surrendered at all by the other.

"Physically speaking, we cannot separate. We cannot remove our respective Sections from each other, nor build an impassable wall between them. A husband and wife may be divorced, and each go out of the presence and beyond the reach of the other; but the different parts of our Country cannot do this. They cannot but remain face to face; and intercourse, either amicable or hostile, must continue between them.

"'Is it possible, then, to make that intercourse more advantageous or more satisfactory after separation than before? Can aliens make treaties easier than friends can make laws? Can treaties be more faithfully enforced between aliens than laws can among friends? suppose you go to War, you cannot fight always; and when, after much loss on both sides, and no gain on either, you cease fighting, the identical old questions as to terms of intercourse are again upon you.'

"There is no line, straight or crooked, suitable for a National boundary upon which to divide. Trace through, from East to West, upon the line between the Free and Slave Country, and we shall find a little more than one third of its length are rivers, easy to be crossed, and populated, or soon to be populated, thickly upon both sides; while nearly all its remaining length are merely surveyors' lines, over which people may walk back and forth without any consciousness of their presence.

"No part of this line can be made any more difficult to pass, by writing it down on paper or parchment as a National boundary. The fact of separation, if it comes, gives up, on the part of the seceding Section, the Fugitive Slave clause, along with all other Constitutional obligations upon the Section seceded from, while I should expect no treaty stipulations would ever be made to take its place.

"But there is another difficulty. The great interior region, bounded East by the Alleghanies, North by the British dominions, West by the Rocky Mountains, and South by the line along which the culture of corn and cotton meets, and which includes part of Virginia, part of Tennessee, all of Kentucky, Ohio, Indiana, Michigan, Wisconsin, Illinois, Missouri, Kansas, Iowa, Minnesota, and the Territories of Dakota, Nebraska, and part of Colorado, already has above ten million people, and will have fifty millions within fifty years, if not prevented by any political folly or mistake.

"It contains more than one-third of the country owned by the United States-certainly more than one million square miles. Once half as populous as Massachusetts already is, it would have more than seventy-five million people. A glance at the map shows that, territorially speaking, it is the great body of the Republic. The other parts are but marginal borders to it, the magnificent region sloping West, from the Rocky Mountains to the Pacific, being the deepest and also the richest in undeveloped resources. In the production of provisions, grains, grasses, and all which proceed from them, this great interior region is naturally one of the most important in the World.

"Ascertain from the statistics the small proportion of the region which has, as yet, been brought into cultivation, and also the large and rapidly increasing amount of its products, and we shall be overwhelmed with the magnitude of the prospect presented. And yet this region has no sea coast, touches no ocean anywhere. As part of one Nation, its people now find, and may forever find, their way to Europe by New York, to South America and Africa by New Orleans, and to Asia by San Francisco.

"But separate our common Country into two nations, as designed by the present Rebellion, and every man of this great interior region is thereby cut off from some one or more of these outlets, not, perhaps, by a physical barrier, but by embarrassing and onerous trade regulations.

"And this is true, wherever a dividing or boundary line may be fixed. Place it between the now Free and Slave country, or place it South of Kentucky, or North of Ohio, and still the truth remains, that none South of it can trade to any port or place North of it, and none North of it can trade to any port or place South of it except upon terms dictated by a Government foreign to them.

"These outlets, East, West, and South, are indispensable to the well-being of the people inhabiting, and to inhabit, this vast interior region. Which of the three may be the best, is no proper question. All, are better than either; and all, of right belong to that People, and to their successors forever. True to themselves, they will not ask where a line of separation shall be, but will vow rather that there shall be no such line.

"Nor are the marginal regions less interested in these communications to and through them, to the great outside World. They too, and each of them, must have access to this Egypt of the West without paying toll at the crossing of any National boundary.

"Our National strife springs not from our permanent part; not from the Land we inhabit; not from our National homestead. There is no possible severing of this, but would multiply, and not mitigate, evils among us. In all its adaptations and aptitudes it demands Union, and abhors separation. In fact it would, ere long, force reunion, however much of blood and treasure the separation might have cost.

"Our strife pertains to ourselves—to the passing generations of men; and it can, without convulsion, be hushed forever—with the passing of one generation.

"In this view I recommend the adoption of the following Resolution and Articles Amendatory of the Constitution of the United States.

"'Resolved by the Senate and House of Representatives of the United States of America, in Congress assembled, (two-thirds of both Houses concurring). That the following Articles be proposed to the Legislatures (or Conventions) of the several States, as Amendments to the Constitution of the United States, all or any of which Articles when ratified by three-fourths of the said Legislatures (or Conventions) to be valid as part or parts of the said Constitution, namely:

"'ARTICLE—Every State wherein Slavery now exists, which shall abolish the same therein, at any time, or times, before the first day of January, in the year of our Lord one thousand nine hundred, shall receive compensation from the United States, as follows, to wit;

"'The President of the United States shall deliver to every such State, bonds of the United States, bearing interest at the rate of per cent. per annum, to an amount equal to the aggregate sum of for each Slave shown to have been therein by the eighth census of the United States, said bonds to be delivered to such States by installments, or in one parcel, at the completion of the abolishment, accordingly as the same shall have been gradual, or at one time, within such State; and interest shall begin to run upon any such bond only from the proper time of its delivery as aforesaid. Any State having received bonds as aforesaid, and afterward reintroducing or tolerating Slavery therein, shall refund to the United States the bonds so received, or the value thereof, and all interest paid thereon.

"'ARTICLE—All Slaves who shall have enjoyed actual freedom by the chances of the War at any time before the end of the Rebellion, shall be forever Free; but all owners of such, who shall not have been disloyal, shall be compensated for them, at the same rates as is provided for States adopting abolishment of Slavery, but in such way that no Slave shall be twice accounted for.

"'ARTICLE—Congress may appropriate money, and otherwise provide for colonizing Free Colored Persons, with their own consent, at any place or places within the United States.'

"I beg indulgence to discuss these proposed Articles at some length. Without Slavery the Rebellion could never have existed; without Slavery it could not continue.

"Among the friends of the Union there is great diversity of sentiment and of policy in regard to Slavery, and the African race among us. Some would perpetuate Slavery; some would abolish it suddenly, without compensation; some would abolish it gradually, and with compensation; some would remove the Freed people from us; and some would retain them with us; and there are yet other minor diversities. Because of these diversities, we waste much strength in struggles among ourselves.

"By mutual Concession we should harmonize and act together. This would be Compromise; but it would be Compromise among the friends, and not with the enemies of the Union. These Articles are intended to embody a plan of such mutual concessions. If the plan shall be adopted, it is assumed that Emancipation will follow, at least, in several of the States.

"As to the first Article, the main points are: first, the Emancipation; secondly, the length of time for consummating it—thirty-seven years; and, thirdly, the compensation.

"The Emancipation will be unsatisfactory to the advocates of perpetual Slavery; but the length of time should greatly mitigate their dissatisfaction. The time spares both races from the evils of sudden derangement—in fact from the necessity of any derangement—while most of those whose habitual course of thought will be disturbed by the measure will have passed away before its consummation. They will never see it.

"Another class will hail the prospect of Emancipation, but will deprecate the length of time. They will feel that it gives too little to the now living Slaves. But it really gives them much. It saves them from the vagrant destitution which must largely attend immediate Emancipation in localities where their numbers are very great; and it gives the inspiring assurance that their posterity shall be Free forever.

"The plan leaves to each State, choosing to act under it, to abolish Slavery now, or at the end of the century, or at any intermediate time, or by degrees, extending over the whole or any part of the period; and it obliges no two States to proceed alike. It also provides for compensation,—and generally, the mode of making it. This, it would seem, must further mitigate the dissatisfaction of those who favor perpetual Slavery, and especially of those who are to receive the compensation. Doubtless some of those who are to pay, and not to receive, will object. Yet the measure is both just and economical.

"In a certain sense, the liberation of Slaves is the destruction of Property—Property acquired by descent, or by purchase, the same as any other property. It is no less true for having been often said, that the people of the South are not more responsible for the original introduction of this Property than are the people of the North; and when it is remembered how unhesitatingly we all use cotton and sugar, and share the profits of dealing in them, it may not be quite safe to say that the South has been more responsible than the North for its continuance.

"If, then, for a common object, this Property is to be sacrificed, is it not just that it be done at a common charge?

"And if, with less money, or money more easily paid, we can preserve the benefits of the Union by this means than we can by the War alone, is it not also economical to do it? Let us consider it then. Let us ascertain the sum we have expended in the War since compensated Emancipation was proposed last March, and consider whether, if that measure had been promptly accepted, by even some of the Slave States, the same sum would not have done more to close the War than has been otherwise done. If so, the measure would save money, and, in that view, would be a prudent and economical measure.

"Certainly it is not so easy to pay something as it is to pay nothing; but it is easier to pay a large sum than it is to pay a larger one. And it is easier to pay any sum when we are able, than it is to pay it before we are able. The War requires large sums, and requires them at once.

"The aggregate sum necessary for compensated Emancipation of course would be large. But it would require no ready cash, nor the bonds, even, any faster than the Emancipation progresses. This might not, and probably would not, close before the end of the thirty-seven years. At that time we shall probably have a hundred million people to share the burden, instead of thirty-one millions, as now. And not only so, but the increase of our population may be expected to continue, for a long time after that period, as rapidly as before; because our territory will not have become full.

"I do not state this inconsiderately. At the same ratio of increase which we have maintained, on an average, from our first National census in 1790, until that of 1860, we should, in 1900, have a population of 103,208,415. And why may we not continue that ratio far beyond that period?

"Our abundant room—our broad National homestead—is our ample resource. Were our territory as limited as are the British Isles, very certainly our population could not expand as stated. Instead of receiving the foreign born, as now, we should be compelled to send part of the Native-born away.

"But such is not our condition. We have two million nine hundred and sixty-three thousand square miles. Europe has three million and eight hundred thousand, with a population averaging seventy-three and one-third persons to the square mile. Why may not our Country at some time, average as many? Is it less fertile? Has it more waste surface by mountains, rivers, lakes, deserts, or other causes? Is it inferior to Europe in any natural advantage?

"If, then, we are at some time to be as populous as Europe, how soon? As to when this may be, we can judge by the past and the present; as to when it will be, if ever, depends much on whether we maintain the Union.

"Several of our States are already above the average of Europe—seventy-three and a third to the square mile. Massachusetts has 157; Rhode Island, 133; Connecticut, 99; New York and New Jersey, each, 80. Also two other great States, Pennsylvania and Ohio, are not far below, the former having 63, and the latter 59. The States already above the European average, except New York, have increased in as rapid a ratio, since passing that point, as ever before; while no one of them is equal to some other parts of our Country in natural capacity for sustaining a dense population.

"Taking the Nation in the aggregate, and we find its population and ratio of increase, for the several decennial periods, to be as follows:

YEAR. POPULATION. RATIO OF INCREASE

1790— 3,929,827
1800— 5,305,937 —35.02 Per Cent.
1810— 7,239,814 —36.45
1820— 9,638,131 —33.13
1830— 12,866,020 —33.49
1840— 17,069,453 —32.67
1850— 23,191,876 —35.87
1860— 31,443,790 —35.58

"This shows an average Decennial Increase of 34.69 per cent. in population through the seventy years from our first to our last census yet taken. It is seen that the ratio of increase, at no one of these seven periods, is either two per cent. below or two per cent. above the average; thus showing how inflexible, and, consequently, how reliable, the law of Increase, in our case, is.

"Assuming that it will continue, gives the following results:

YEAR. POPULATION.

1870— 42,323,041
1880— 56,967,216
1890— 76,677,872
1900— 103,208,415
1910— 138,918,526
1920— 186,984,335
1930— 251,680,914

"These figures show that our Country may be as populous as Europe now is at some point between 1920 and 1930—say about 1925—our territory, at seventy-three and a third persons to the square mile, being of capacity to contain 217,186,000.

"And we will reach this, too, if we do not ourselves relinquish the chance by the folly and evils of Disunion or by long and exhausting War springing from the only great element of National discord among us. While it cannot be foreseen exactly how much one huge example of Secession, breeding lesser ones indefinitely, would retard population, civilization and prosperity, no one can doubt that the extent of it would be very great and injurious.

"The proposed Emancipation would shorten the War, perpetuate Peace, insure this increase of population, and proportionately the wealth of the Country. With these, we should pay all the Emancipation would cost, together with our other debt, easier than we should pay our other debt without it.

"If we had allowed our old National debt to run at six per cent. per annum, simple interest, from the end of our Revolutionary Struggle until to-day, without paying anything on either principal or interest, each man of us would owe less upon that debt now than each man owed upon it then; and this because our increase of men through the whole period has been greater than six per cent.; has run faster than the interest upon the debt. Thus, time alone, relieves a debtor Nation, so long as its population increases faster than unpaid interest accumulates on its debt.

"This fact would be no excuse for delaying payment of what is justly due, but it shows the great importance of time in this connection—the great advantage of a policy by which we shall not have to pay until we number a hundred millions, what, by a different policy, we would have to pay now, when we number but thirty-one millions. In a word, it shows that a dollar will be much harder to pay for the War, than will be a dollar for Emancipation on the proposed plan. And then the latter will cost no blood, no precious life. It will be a saving of both.

"As to the Second Article, I think it would be impracticable to return to Bondage the class of Persons therein contemplated. Some of them, doubtless, in the property sense, belong to loyal owners and hence provision is made in this Article for compensating such.

"The Third Article relates to the future of the Freed people. It does not oblige, but merely authorizes, Congress to aid in colonizing such as may consent. This ought not to be regarded as objectionable on the one hand or on the other, insomuch as it comes to nothing, unless by the mutual consent of the people to be deported, and the American voters, through their Representatives in Congress.

"I cannot make it better known than it already is, that I strongly favor colonization. And yet I wish to say there is an objection urged against free Colored persons remaining in the Country which is largely imaginary, if not sometimes malicious.

"It is insisted that their presence would injure and displace White labor and White laborers. If there ever could be a proper time for mere catch arguments, that time surely is not now. In times like the present men should utter nothing for which they would not willingly be responsible through Time and in Eternity.

"Is it true, then, that Colored people can displace any more White labor by being Free, than by remaining Slaves? If they stay in their old places, they jostle no White laborers; if they leave their old places, they leave them open to White laborers. Logically, there is neither more nor less of it.

"Emancipation, even without deportation, would probably enhance the wages of White labor, and, very surely would not reduce them. Thus, the customary amount of labor would still have to be performed; the freed people would surely not do more than their old proportion of it and, very probably, for a time would do less, leaving an increased part to White laborers, bringing their labor into greater demand, and consequently enhancing the wages of it.

"With deportation, even to a limited extent, enhanced wages to White labor is mathematically certain. Labor is like any other commodity in the market-

increase the demand for it and you increase the price of it. Reduce the supply of Black labor by colonizing the Black laborer out of the Country, and by precisely so much you increase the demand for and wages of White labor.

"But it is dreaded that the freed people will swarm forth and cover the whole Land! Are they not already in the Land? Will liberation make them any more numerous? Equally distributed among the Whites of the whole Country, there would be but one Colored, in seven Whites. Could the one, in any way, greatly disturb the seven?

"There are many communities now, having more than one free Colored person to seven Whites; and this, without any apparent consciousness of evil from it. The District of Columbia, and the States of Maryland and Delaware, are all in this condition. The District has more than one free Colored to six Whites; and yet, in its frequent petitions to Congress I believe it has never presented the presence of free Colored persons as one of its grievances.

"But why should Emancipation South, send the freed people North? people of any color, seldom run, unless there be something to run from. Heretofore, Colored people, to some extent, have fled North from bondage, and now, perhaps, from both bondage and destitution. But if gradual Emancipation and deportation be adopted, they will have neither to flee from.

"Their old masters will give them wages at least until new laborers can be procured; and the freed men, in turn, will gladly give their labor for the wages, till new homes can be found for them, in congenial climes, and with people of their own blood and race.

"This proposition can be trusted on the mutual interests involved. And, in any event, cannot the North decide for itself, whether to receive them?

"Again, as practice proves more than theory, in any case, has there been any irruption of Colored people Northward because of the abolishment of Slavery in this District last Spring? What I have said of the proportion of free Colored persons to the Whites in the District is from the census of 1860, having no reference to persons called Contrabands, nor to those made free by the Act of Congress abolishing Slavery here.

"The plan consisting of these Articles is recommended, not but that a restoration of the National authority would be accepted without its adoption.

"Nor will the War, nor proceedings under the Proclamation of September 22, 1862, be stayed because of the recommendation of this plan. Its timely adoption, I doubt not, would bring restoration, and thereby stay both.

"And, notwithstanding this plan, the recommendation that Congress provides by law for compensating any State which may adopt Emancipation before this plan shall have been acted upon, is hereby earnestly renewed.

Such would be only an advance part of the plan, and the same arguments apply to both.

"This plan is recommended as a means, not in exclusion of, but additional to, all others, for restoring and preserving the National authority throughout the Union. The subject is presented exclusively in its economical aspect.

"The plan would, I am confident, secure Peace more speedily, and maintain it more permanently, than can be done by force alone; while all it would cost, considering amounts, and manner of payment, and times of payment, would be easier paid than will be the additional cost of the War, if we rely solely upon force. It is much, very much, that it would cost no blood at all.

"The plan is proposed as permanent Constitutional Law. It cannot become such without the concurrence of, first, two-thirds of Congress, and afterward, three-fourths of the Slave States. The requisite three-fourths of the States will necessarily include seven of the Slave States. Their concurrence, if obtained, will give assurance of their severally adopting Emancipation at no very distant day upon the new Constitutional terms. This assurance would end the struggle now and save the Union forever.

"I do not forget the gravity which should characterize a paper addressed to the Congress of the Nation by the Chief Magistrate of the Nation. Nor do I forget that some of you are my seniors, nor that many of you have more experience than I in the conduct of public affairs. Yet I trust that in view of the great responsibility resting upon me, you will perceive no want of respect to yourselves in any undue earnestness I may seem to display.

"Is it doubted, then, that the plan I propose, if adopted, would shorten the War, and thus lessen its expenditure of money and of blood? Is it doubted that it would restore the National authority and National prosperity, and perpetuate both indefinitely? Is it doubted that we here—Congress and Executive—can secure its adoption; will not the good people respond to a united and earnest appeal from us? Can we, can they, by any other means so certainly or so speedily assure these vital objects; we can succeed only by concert.

"It is not, 'Can any of us imagine better?' but,'Can we all do better?' Object whatsoever is possible, still the question recurs, 'Can we do better? The dogmas of the quiet past are inadequate to the stormy present. The occasion is piled high with difficulty, and we must rise with the occasion. As our case is new, so we must think anew, and act anew. We must disenthrall ourselves, and then we shall save our Country.

"Fellow-citizens, we cannot escape history. We, of this Congress and this Administration, will be remembered in spite of ourselves. No personal significance, or insignificance, can spare one or another of us. The fiery trial through which we pass will light us down in honor or dishonor, to the latest generation.

"We say we are for the Union. The World will not forget that we say this. We know how to save the Union.

"The World knows we do know how to save it. We even we here—hold the power, and bear the responsibility.

"In giving Freedom to the Slave, we assure Freedom to the Free-Honorable alike in what we give and what we preserve. We shall nobly save, or meanly lose, the last, best hope of Earth. Other means may succeed; this could not fail. The way is plain, peaceful, generous, just—a way which, if followed, the World would forever applaud, and God must forever bless.

"ABRAHAM LINCOLN."

The popular Branch of Congress responded with heartiness to what Mr. Lincoln had done. On December 11, 1862, resolutions were offered by Mr. Yeaman in the House of Representatives, as follows:

"Resolved by the House of Representatives (the Senate Concurring), That the Proclamation of the President of the United States, of date the 22d of September, 1862, is not warranted by the Constitution.

"Resolved, That the policy of Emancipation as indicated in that Proclamation, is not calculated to hasten the restoration of Peace, was not well chosen as a War measure, and is an assumption of power dangerous to the rights of citizens and to the perpetuity of a Free People."

These resolutions were laid on the table by 95 yeas to 47 nays—the yeas all Republicans, save three, and the nays all Democrats save five.

On December 15, 1862, Mr. S. C. Fessenden, of Maine, offered resolutions to the House, in these words:

"Resolved, That the Proclamation of the President of the United States, of the date of 22d September, 1862, is warranted by the Constitution.

"Resolved, That the policy of Emancipation, as indicated in that Proclamation, is well adapted to hasten the restoration of Peace, was well chosen as a War measure, and is an exercise of power with proper regard for the rights of the States, and the perpetuity of Free Government."

These resolutions were adopted by 78 yeas to 52 nays—the yeas all Republicans, save two, and the nays all Democrats, save seven.

The Proclamation of September 22d, 1862, was very generally endorsed and upheld by the People at large; and, in accordance with its promise, it was followed at the appointed time, January 1st, 1863, by the supplemental Proclamation specifically Emancipating the Slaves in the rebellious parts of the United States—in the following terms:

"WHEREAS, On the twenty-second day of September, in the year of our Lord one thousand eight hundred and sixty-two, a Proclamation was issued by the President of the United States, containing, among other things, the following, to wit:

"'That on the first day of January, in the year of our Lord one thousand eight hundred and sixty-three, all Persons held as Slaves within any State, or designated part of a State, the people whereof shall then be in Rebellion against the United States, shall be then, thenceforward, and forever Free; and the Executive Government of the United States, including the Military and Naval Authority thereof, will recognize and maintain the Freedom of such Persons, and will do no act or acts to repress such Persons, or any of them, in any efforts they may make for their actual Freedom.

"'That the Executive will, on the First day of January aforesaid, by Proclamation, designate the States and parts of States, if any, in which the people thereof, respectively, shall then be in Rebellion against the United States; and the fact that any State, or the people thereof, shall on that day be in good faith represented in the Congress of the United States, by members chosen thereto at elections wherein a majority of the qualified voters of such States shall have participated, shall, in the absence of strong countervailing testimony, be deemed conclusive evidence that such State, and the people thereof, are not then in Rebellion against the United States.'

"Now, therefore, I ABRAHAM LINCOLN, President of the United States, by virtue of the power in me vested as Commander-in-Chief of the Army and Navy of the United States, in time of actual armed Rebellion against the authority and Government of the United States, and as a fit and necessary War measure for suppressing said Rebellion, do, on this First day of January, in the Year of Our Lord one thousand eight hundred and sixty-three, and in accordance with my purpose so to do, publicly proclaimed for the full period of one hundred days from the day first above mentioned, Order and designate as the States and parts of States wherein the people thereof, respectively, are this day in Rebellion against the United States, the following, to wit:

"Arkansas, Texas, Louisiana (except the parishes of St. Bernard, Plaquemines, Jefferson, St. John, St. Charles, St. James, Ascension, Assumption, Terre Bonne, Lafouche, St. Mary, St. Martin, and Orleans, including the City of New Orleans,) Mississippi, Alabama, Florida, Georgia, South Carolina, North Carolina, and Virginia, (except the forty-eight counties designated as West Virginia, and also the counties of Berkeley, Accomac, Northampton, Elizabeth City, York, Princess Ann, and Norfolk, including the cities of Norfolk and Portsmouth), and which excepted parts are for the present left precisely as if this Proclamation were not issued.

"And by virtue of the power and for the purpose aforesaid, I do Order and declare that all Persons held as Slaves within said designated States and parts of States are, and henceforward shall be, Free; and that the Executive Government of the United States, including the Military and Naval authorities thereof; will recognize and maintain the Freedom of said Persons.

"And I hereby enjoin upon the people so declared to be Free, to abstain from all violence, unless in necessary self-defence; and I recommend to them that, in all cases when allowed, they labor faithfully for reasonable wages.

"And I further declare and make known that such Persons, of suitable condition, will be received into the armed service of the United States to garrison forts, positions, stations, and other places, and to man vessels of all sorts in said service.

"And upon this act, sincerely believed to be an act of justice, warranted by the Constitution upon Military necessity, I invoke the considerate judgment of mankind and the gracious favor of Almighty God.

"In witness whereof, I have hereunto set my hand, and caused the seal of the United States to be affixed.

"Done at the City of Washington, this First day of January, in the year of Our Lord one thousand eight hundred and sixty-three, and of the Independence of the United States of America the eighty-seventh.

"By the President:

"ABRAHAM LINCOLN.

"WILLIAM H. SEWARD, Secretary of State."

HISTORICAL REVIEW

Let us now refresh recollection by glancing backward over the history of our Country, and we shall see, as recorded in these pages, that, from the first, there existed in this Nation a class of individuals greedily ambitious of power and determined to secure and maintain control of this Government; that they left unturned no stone which would contribute to the fostering and to the extension of African Slavery; that, hand in hand with African Slavery—and as a natural corollary to it—they advocated Free Trade as a means of degrading Free White labor to the level of Black Slave labor, and thus increasing their own power; that from the first, ever taking advantage of the general necessities of the Union, they arrogantly demanded and received from a brow-beaten People, concession after concession, and compromise after compromise; that every possible pretext and occasion was seized by them to increase, consolidate, and secure their power, and to extend the territorial limits over which their peculiar Pro-Slavery and Pro-Free-Trade doctrines prevailed; and that their nature was so exacting, and their greed so rapacious, that it was impossible ever to satisfy them.

Nor were they burdened with over-much of that high sense of honor—a quality of which they often vaunted themselves—which impelled others to stand by their agreements. It seemed as though they considered the most sacred promises and covenants of no account, and made only to be trampled upon, when in the way of their Moloch.

We remember the bitter Slavery agitation in Congress over the admission of the State of Missouri, and how it eventuated in the Missouri Compromise. That compromise, we have seen, they afterward trod upon, and broke, with as little compunction as they would have stepped upon and crushed a toad.

They felt their own growing power, and gloried in their strength and arrogance; and Northern timidity became a scoff and by-word in their mouths.

33

The fact is, that from its very conception, as well as birth, they hated and opposed the Union, because they disliked a Republican and preferred a Monarchical form of Government. Their very inability to prevent the consummation of that Union, imbittered them. Hence their determination to seize every possible occasion and pretext afterward to destroy it, believing, as they doubtless did, that upon the crumbled and mouldering ruins of a dissevered Union and ruptured Republic, Monarchical ideas might the more easily take root and grow. But experience had already taught them that it would be long before their real object could even be covertly hinted at, and that in the meantime it must be kept out of sight by the agitation of other political issues. The formulation and promulgation therefore, by Jefferson, in the Kentucky Resolutions of 1798, and by Madison, in the Virginia Resolutions of 1799, of the doctrine of States Rights already referred to, was a perfect "God-send" to these men. For it not only enabled them to keep from public view and knowledge their ultimate aim and purpose, but constituted the whip which they thenceforth everlastingly flourished and cracked over the shrinking heads of other and more patriotic people—the whip with which, through the litter of their broken promises, they ruthlessly rode into, and, for so long a period of years held on to, supreme power and place in the Land.

Including within the scope of States Rights, the threats of Nullification, Disunion and Secession—ideas abhorrent to the Patriot's mind—small wonder is it that, in those days, every fresh demand made by these political autocrats was tremblingly acceded to, until patience and concession almost utterly exhausted themselves.

Originally disturbing only South Carolina and Georgia to any extent, these ambitious men, who believed in anything rather than a Republic, and who were determined to destroy the Union, gradually spread the spirit of jealousy and discontent into other States of the South; their immediate object being to bring the Southern States into the closest possible relations the one with the other; to inspire them all with common sympathies and purposes; to compact and solidify them, so that in all coming movements against the other States of the Union, they might move with proportionately increased power, and force, and effect, because of such unity of aim and strength.

This spirit of Southern discontent, and jealousy of the Northern States, was, as we have seen, artfully fanned by the Conspirators, in heated discussions over the Tariff Acts of 1824, and 1828, and 1832, until, by the latter date, the people of the Cotton-States were almost frantic, and ready to fight over their imaginary grievances. Then it was that the Conspirators thought the time had come, for which they had so long and so earnestly prayed and worked, when the cotton Sampson should wind his strong arms around the pillars of the Constitution and pull down the great Temple of our Union—

that they might rear upon its site another and a stronger edifice, dedicated not to Freedom, but to Free-Trade and to other false gods.

South Carolina was to lead off, and the other Cotton States would follow. South Carolina did lead off—but the other Cotton-States did not follow.

It has been shown in these pages how South Carolina declared the Tariff Acts aforesaid, null and void, armed herself to resist force, and declared that any attempt of the general Government to enforce those Acts would cause her to withdraw from the Union. But Jackson as we know throttled the treason with so firm a grip that Nullification and Secession and Disunion were at once paralyzed.

The concessions to the domineering South, in Clay's Compromise Tariff of 1833, let the Conspirators down easily, so to speak; and they pretended to be satisfied. But they were satisfied only as are the thirsty sands of Africa with the passing shower.

The Conspirators had, however, after all, made substantial gains. They had established a precedent for an attempt to secede. That was something. They had demonstrated that a single Southern State could stand up, armed and threatening, strutting, blustering, and bullying, and at least make faces at the general Government without suffering any very dreadful consequences. That was still more.

They had also ascertained that, by adopting such a course, a single Southern State could force concessions from the fears of the rest of the United States. That was worth knowing, because the time might come, when it might be desirable not only for one but for all the Southern States to secede upon some other pretext, and when it would be awkward, and would interfere with the Disunion programme, to have the other States either offer or make concessions.

They had also learned the valuable lesson that the single issue of Free-Trade was not sufficiently strong of itself to unite all the Southern States in a determination to secede, and thus dissolve the Union. They saw they must agitate some other issue to unify the South more thoroughly and justify Disunion. On looking over the whole field they concluded that the Slavery question would best answer their purpose, and they adopted it.

It was doubtless a full knowledge of the fact that they had adopted it, that led Jackson to make the declaration, heretofore in these pages given, which has been termed "prophetic." At any rate, thenceforth the programme of the Conspirators was to agitate the Slavery question in all ways possible, so as to increase, extend and solidify the influence and strength of the Slave power; strain the bonds uniting them with the Free States; and weaken the Free States by dividing them upon the question. At the same time the Free-Trade question was to be pressed forward to a triumphal issue, so that the South might be enriched and strengthened, and the North impoverished and weakened, by the result.

That was their programme, in the rough, and it was relentlessly adhered to. Free-Trade and Slavery by turns, if not together, from that time onward, were ever at the front, agitating our People both North and South, and not only consolidating the Southern States on those lines, as the Conspirators designed, but also serving ultimately to consolidate, to some extent—in a manner quite unlooked for by the Conspirators—Northern sentiment, on the opposite lines of Protection and Freedom.

The Compromise Tariff Act of 1833—which Clay was weak enough to concede, and even stout old Jackson to permit to become law without his signature—gave to the Conspirators great joy for years afterward, as they witnessed the distress and disaster brought by it to Northern homes and incomes—not distress and disaster alone, but absolute and apparently irreparable ruin.

The reaction occasioned by this widespread ruin having brought the Whigs into power, led to the enactment of the Protective-Tariff of 1842 and—to the chagrin of the Conspirators—industrial prosperity and plenty to the Free North again ensued.

Even as Cain hated his brother Abel because his sacrifices were acceptable in the sight of God, while his own were not, so the Southern Conspirators, and other Slave-owners also, had, by this time, come to hate the Northern free-thinking, free-acting, freedom-loving mechanic and laboring man, because the very fact and existence of his Godgiven Freedom and higher-resulting civilization was a powerful and perpetual protest against the— abounding iniquities and degradations of Slavery as practiced by themselves. Hence, by trickery, by cajoling the People With his, and their own, assurances that he was in favor of Protection—they secured the election in 1844 of a Free-Trade President, the consequent repeal of the Protective-Tariff of 1842—which had repaired the dreadful mischief wrought by the Compromise Act of 1833—and the enactment of the infamous Free-Trade Tariff of 1846, which blasted the manufacturing and farming and trade industries of the Country again, as with fire.

The discovery of the great gold fields of California, and the enormous amount of the precious metal poured by her for many succeeding years into the lap of the Nation, alone averted what otherwise would inevitably have been total ruin. As it was, in 1860, the National credit had sunk to a lower point than ever before in all its history. It was confessedly bankrupt, and ruin stalked abroad throughout the United States.

But while, with rapid pen, the carrying out of that part of the Southern Conspirators' Disunion programme which related to Free-Trade, is thus brought again to mind, the other part of that programme, which related to Slavery, must not be neglected or overlooked. On this question they had determined, as we have seen, to agitate without ceasing—having in view, primarily, as already hinted, the extension of Slave territory and the resulting increase of Slave power in the Land; and, ulteriorly, the solidifying of that power, and Disunion of the Republic, with a view to its conversion into an Oligarchy, if not a Monarchy.

The bitterness of the struggle over the admission of Missouri as a Slave State in 1820, under the Missouri Compromise, was to be revived by the Conspirators, at the earliest possible moment.

Accordingly in 1836—only three years after the failure of Nullification in South Carolina, the Territory, of Arkansas was forced in as a Slave State, and simultaneously the Slave-owning henchmen of the Conspirators, previously settled there for the purpose, proclaimed the secession from Mexico, and independence, of Texas. This was quickly followed, in 1844, by Calhoun's hastily negotiated treaty of annexation with Texas; its miscarriage in the Senate; and the Act of March 2, 1845—with its sham compromise—consenting to the admission of Texas to the Union of States.

Then came the War with Mexico; the attempt by means of the Wilmot proviso to check the growing territorial-greed and rapacity of the Slave-power; and the acquisition by the United States, of California and New Mexico, under the treaty of Guadalupe Hidalgo in 1848, which brought Peace.

Then occurred the agitation over the organization of Territorial governments for Oregon, California, and New Mexico, and the strong effort to extend to the Pacific Ocean the Missouri-Compromise line of 36 30', and to extend to all future Territorial organizations the principles of that compromise.

Then came the struggle in 1850, over the admission of California as a State, and New Mexico and Utah to Territorial organization—ending in the passage of Clay's Compromise measures of 1850.

Yet still the Southern Conspirators—whose forces, both in Congress and out, were now well-disciplined, compacted, solidified, experienced, and bigotedly enthusiastic and overbearing—were not satisfied. It was not their intention to be satisfied with anything less than the destruction of the Union and of our Republican form of Government. The trouble was only beginning, and, so far, almost everything had progressed to their liking. The work must proceed.

In 1852-3 they commenced the Kansas-Nebraska agitation; and, what with their incessant political and colonizing movements in those Territories; the frequent and dreadful atrocities committed by their tools, the Border-ruffians; the incessant turmoil created by cruelties to their Fugitive-slaves; their persistent efforts to change the Supreme Court to their notions; these—with the decision and opinion of the Supreme Court in the Dred Scott case—together worked the Slavery question up to a dangerous degree of heat, by the year 1858.

And, by 1860—when the people of the Free States, grown sick unto death of the rule of the Slave-power in the General Government, arose in their political might, and shook off this "Old Man of the Sea," electing, beyond cavil and by the Constitutional mode, to the Presidential office, a man who thoroughly represented in himself their conscience, on the one hand, which instinctively revolted against human Slavery as a wrong committed against the laws of God, and their sense of justice and equity on the other, which would not lightly overlook, or interfere with vested rights under the Constitution and the laws of man—the Conspirators had reached the point at which they had been aiming ever since that failure in 1832 of their first attempt at Disunion, in South Carolina.

They had now succeeded in irritating both the Free and the Slave-holding Sections of our Country against each other, to an almost unbearable point; had solidified the Southern States on the Slavery and Free-Trade questions; and at last—the machinations of these same Conspirators having resulted in a split in the Democratic Party, and the election of the Republican candidate to the Presidency, as the embodiment of the preponderating National belief in Freedom and equality to all before the Law, with Protection to both Labor and Capital—they also had the pretext for which they had both been praying and scheming and preparing all those long, long years—they, and some of their fathers before them.

It cannot be too often repeated that to secure a Monarchy, or at least an Oligarchy, over which the leading Conspirators should rule for life—whether that Monarchy or that Oligarchy should comprise the States of the South by themselves, or all the States on a new basis of Union—was the great ultimate aim of the Conspirators; and this could be secured only by first disrupting the then existing Republican Union of Republican States.

The doctrine of the right of Secession had now long been taught, and had become a part of the Southern Slave-holders' Democratic creed, as fully as had the desirability of Slavery and Free-Trade—and even many of the Northern Democrats, and some Republicans as well, were not much inclined to dispute, although they cared not to canvass, the point.

The programme of action was therefore much the same as had been laid down in the first attempt in 1832:—first South Carolina would secede and declare her independence; then the other Slave States in quick succession would do likewise; then a new Constitution for a solid Southern Union; then, if necessary, a brief War to cement it—which would end, of course, in the independence of the South at least, but more probably in the utter subjugation and humiliation of the Free States.

When the time should come, during, or after this War—as come, in their belief, it would—for a change in the form of Government, then they could seize the first favorable occasion and change it. At present, however, the cry must be for "independence." That accomplished, the rest would be easy. And until that independence was accomplished, no terms of any sort, no settlement of any kind, were either to be proposed or accepted by them.

These were their dreams, their ambitions, their plans; and the tenacious courage with which they stuck to them "through thick and thin," through victory and disaster, were worthy of a better cause.

While, therefore, the pretexts for Secession were "Slavery" and "Free-Trade"—both of which were alleged to be jeopardized in the election and inauguration of Abraham Lincoln—yet, no sooner had hostilities commenced between the seceding States and the Union, than they declared to the World that their fight was not for Slavery, but for Independence.

They dared not acknowledge to the World that they fought for Slavery, lest the sympathies of the World should be against them. But it was well understood by the Southern masses, as well as the other people of the Union, that both Slavery and Free-Trade were involved in the fight—as much as independence, and the consequent downfall of the Union.

President Lincoln, however, had made up his mind to do all he properly could to placate the South. None knew better than he, the history of this Secession movement, as herein described. None knew better than he, the fell purpose and spirit of the Conspirators. Yet still, his kindly heart refused to believe that the madness of the Southern leaders was so frenzied, and their hatred of Free men, Free labor, and Free institutions, so implacable, that they would wilfully refuse to listen to reason and ever insist on absolutely inadmissible terms of reconciliation.

From the very beginning of his Administration, he did all that was possible to mollify their resentment and calm their real or pretended fears. Nor was this from any dread or doubt as to what the outcome of an armed Conflict would be; for, in his speech at Cincinnati, in the Autumn of 1859, he had said, while addressing himself to Kentuckians and other Southern men: "Why, gentlemen, I think you are as gallant and as brave men as live; that you can fight as bravely in a good cause, man for man, as any other people living; that you have shown yourselves capable of this upon various occasions; but man for man, you are not better than we are, and there are not so many of you as there are of us. You will never make much of a hand at whipping us. If we were fewer in numbers than you, I think that you could whip us; if we were equal it would likely be a drawn battle; but being inferior in numbers, you will make nothing by attempting to master us."

And early in 1860, in his famous New York Cooper Institute speech he had said "Let us have faith that right makes might, and in that faith, let us, to the end, dare to do our duty as we understand it." He plainly believed to the end, that "right makes might;" and he believed in the power of numbers— as also did Napoleon, if we may judge from his famous declaration that "The God of battles is always on the side of the heaviest battalions." Yet, so believing, President Lincoln exerted himself in all possible ways to mollify the South. His assurances, however, were far from satisfying the

Conspirators. They never had been satisfied with anything in the shape of concession. They never would be. They had been dissatisfied with and had broken all the compacts and compromises, and had spit upon all the concessions, of the past; and nothing would now satisfy them, short of the impossible.

They were not satisfied now with Lincoln's promise that the Government would not assail them—organized as, by this time, they were into a so-called Southern "Confederacy" of States—and they proceeded accordingly to assail that Government which would not assail them. They opened fire on Fort Sumter.

This was done, as has duly appeared, in the hope that the shedding of blood would not only draw the States of the Southern Confederacy more closely together in their common cause, and prevent the return of any of them to their old allegiance, but also to so influence the wavering allegiance to the Union, of the Border States, as to strengthen that Confederacy and equivalently weaken that Union, by their Secession.

Virginia, North Carolina, Tennessee, and Arkansas, of the Border States that were wavering, were thus gathered into the Confederate fold, by this policy of blood-spilling—carried bodily thither, by a desperate and frenzied minority, against the wishes of a patriotic majority.

Virginia, especially, was a great accession to the Rebel cause. She brought to it the prestige of her great name. To secure the active cooperation of "staid old Virginia," "the Mother of Statesmen," in the struggle, was, in the estimation of the Rebels, an assurance of victory to their cause. And the Secession of Virginia for a time had a depressing influence upon the friends of the Union everywhere.

The refusal of West Virginia to go with the rest of the State into Rebellion, was, to be sure, some consolation; and the checkmating of the Conspirators' designs to secure to the Confederacy the States of Maryland, Kentucky and Missouri, helped the confidence of Union men. In fact, as long as the National Capital was secure, it was felt that the Union was still safe.

But while the Confederacy, by the firing upon Fort Sumter, and thus assailing that Government which Lincoln had promised would not assail the Rebels, had gained much in securing the aid of the States mentioned, yet the Union Cause, by that very act, had gained more. For the echoes of the Rebel guns of Fort Moultrie were the signal for such an uprising of the Patriots of the North and West and Middle States, as, for the moment, struck awe to the hearts of Traitors and inspired with courage and hopefulness the hearts of Union men throughout the Land.

Moreover it put the Rebels in their proper attitude, in the eyes of the World—as the first aggressors—and thus deprived them, to a certain extent, of that moral support from the outside which flows from sympathy.

Those echoes were the signal, not only of that call to arms which led to such an uprising, but for the simultaneous calling together of the Thirty-seventh Congress of the United States in Extra Session—the Congress whose measures ultimately enabled President Lincoln and the Union Armies to subdue the Rebellion and save the Union—the Congress whose wise and patriotic deliberations resulted in the raising of those gigantic Armies and Navies, and in supplying the unlimited means, through the Tariff and National Bank Systems and otherwise, by which those tremendous Forces could be both created and effectively operated—the Congress which cooperated with President Lincoln and those Forces in preparing the way for the destruction of the very corner-stone of the Confederacy, Slavery itself.

LINCOLN'S TROUBLES AND TEMPTATIONS

The Rebels themselves, as has already been noted, by the employment of their Slaves in the construction of earthworks and other fortifications, and even in battle, at Bull Run and elsewhere, against the Union Forces, brought the Thirty-seventh Congress, as well as the Military Commanders, and the President, to an early consideration of the Slavery question. But it was none the less a question to be treated with the utmost delicacy.

The Union men, as well as the Secession-sympathizers, of Kentucky and Tennessee and Missouri and Maryland, largely believed in Slavery, or at least were averse to any interference with it. These, would not see that the right to destroy that unholy Institution could pertain to any authority, or be justified by any exigency; much less that, as held by some authorities, its existence ceased at the moment when its hands, or those of the State in which it had existed, were used to assail the General Government.

They looked with especial suspicion and distrust upon the guarded utterances of the President upon all questions touching the future of the Colored Race.

[At Faneuil Hall, Edward Everett is reported to have said, in October of 1864:

"It is very doubtful whether any act of the Government of the United States was necessary to liberate the Slaves in a State which is in Rebellion. There is much reason for the opinion that, by the simple act of levying War against the United States, the relation of Slavery was terminated; certainly, so far as concerns the duty of the United States to recognize it, or to refrain from interfering with it.

"Not being founded on the Law of Nature, and resting solely on positive Local Law—and that, not of the United States—as soon as it becomes either the motive or pretext of an unjust War against the Union—an

43

efficient instrument in the hands of the Rebels for carrying on the War—source of Military strength to the Rebellion, and of danger to the Government at home and abroad, with the additional certainty that, in any event but its abandonment, it will continue, in all future time to work these mischiefs, who can suppose it is the duty of the United States to continue to recognize it.

"To maintain this would be a contradiction in terms. It would be two recognize a right in a Rebel master to employ his Slave in acts of Rebellion and Treason, and the duty of the Slave to aid and abet his master in the commission of the greatest crime known to the Law. No such absurdity can be admitted; and any citizen of the United States, from thee President down, who should, by any overt act, recognize the duty of a Slave to obey a Rebel master in a hostile operation, would himself be giving aid and comfort to the Enemy."]

They believed that when Fremont issued the General Order—heretofore given in full—in which that General declared that "The property, real and personal, of all persons, in the State of Missouri, who shall take up arms against the United States, or who shall be directly proven to have taken an active part with their enemies in the field, is declared to be confiscated to the public use, and their Slaves, if any they have, are hereby declared Free men," it must have been with the concurrence, if not at the suggestion, of the President; and, when the President subsequently, September 11,1861, made an open Order directing that this clause of Fremont's General Order, or proclamation, should be "so modified, held, and construed, as to conform to, and not to transcend, the provisions on the same subject contained in the Act of Congress entitled 'An Act to Confiscate Property used for Insurrectionary Purposes,' approved August 6, 1861," they still were not satisfied.

[The sections of the above Act, bearing upon the matter, are the first and fourth, which are in these words:

"That if, during the present or any future insurrection against the Government of the United States, after the President of the United States shall have declared, by proclamation, that the laws of the United States are opposed, and the execution thereof obstructed, by combinations too powerful to be suppressed by the ordinary course of judicial proceedings, or by the power vested in the marshals by law, any person or persons, his, her, or their agent, attorney, or employee, shall purchase or acquire, sell or give, any property of whatsoever kind or description, with intent to use or employ the same, or suffer the same to be used or employed, in aiding, abetting, or promoting such insurrection or resistance to the laws, or any persons engaged therein; or if any person or persons, being the owner or owners of any such property, shall knowingly use or employ, or consent to the use or employment of the same as aforesaid, all such property is hereby declared to be lawful subject of prize and capture wherever found; and it shall be the duty of the President of the United States to cause the same to be seized, confiscated and condemned."

* * * * * * * *

"SEC. 4. That whenever hereafter, during the present insurrection against the Government of the United States, any person claimed to be held to Labor or Service under the law of any State shall be required or permitted by the person to whom such Labor or Service is claimed to be due, or by the lawful agent of such person, to take up arms against the United States; or shall be required or permitted by the person to whom such Labor or Service is claimed to be due, or his lawful agent, to work or to be employed in or upon any fort, navy-yard, dock, armory, ship, entrenchment, or in any Military or Naval service whatsoever, against the Government and lawful authority of the United States, then, and in every such case, the person to whom such Labor or Service is claimed to be due, shall forfeit his claim to such Labor, any law of the State or of the United States to the contrary notwithstanding. And whenever thereafter the person claiming such Labor or Service shall seek to enforce his claim, it shall be a full and sufficient answer to such claim that the person whose Service or Labor is claimed had been employed in hostile service against the Government of the United States, contrary to the provisions of this act."

It seemed as impossible to satisfy these Border-State men as it had been to satisfy the Rebels themselves.

The Act of Congress, to which President Lincoln referred in his Order modifying Fremont's proclamation, had itself been opposed by them, under the lead of their most influential Representative and spokesman, Mr. Crittenden, of Kentucky, in its passage through that Body. It did not satisfy them.

Neither had they been satisfied, when, within one year and four days after "Slavery opened its batteries of Treason, upon Fort Sumter," that National curse and shame was banished from the Nation's Capital by Congressional enactment.

They were not satisfied even with Mr. Lincoln's conservative suggestions embodied in the Supplemental Act.

Nor were they satisfied with the General Instructions, of October 14, 1861, from the War Department to its Generals, touching the employment of Fugitive Slaves within the Union Lines, and the assurance of just compensation to loyal masters, therein contained, although all avoidable interference with the Institution was therein reprobated.

Nothing satisfied them. It was indeed one of the most curious of the many phenomena of the War of the Rebellion, that when—as at the end of 1861—it had become evident, as Secretary Cameron held, that it "would be National suicide" to leave the Rebels in "peaceful and secure possession of

45

Slave Property, more valuable and efficient to them for War, than forage, cotton, and Military stores," and that the Slaves coming within our lines could not "be held by the Government as Slaves," and should not be held as prisoners of War—still the loyal people of these Border-States, could not bring themselves to save that Union, which they professed to love, by legislation on this tender subject.

On the contrary, they opposed all legislation looking to any interference with such Slave property. Nothing that was proposed by Mr. Lincoln, or any other, on this subject, could satisfy them.

Congress enacted a law, approved March 13, 1862, embracing an additional Article of War, which prohibited all officers "from employing any of the forces under their respective Commands for the purpose of returning Fugitives from Service or Labor who may have escaped from any persons to whom such Service or Labor is claimed to be due," and prescribed that "Any officer who shall be found guilty by Court-Martial of violating this Article shall be dismissed from the Service." In both Houses, the loyal Border-State Representatives spoke and voted against its passage.

One week previously (March 6, 1862), President Lincoln, in an admirable Message, hitherto herein given at length, found himself driven to broach to Congress the subject of Emancipation. He had, in his First Annual Message (December, 1861), declared that "the Union must be preserved; and hence all indispensable means must be employed;" but now, as a part of the War Policy, he proposed to Congress the adoption of a Joint Resolution declaring "That the United States ought to cooperate with any State which may adopt gradual abolishment of Slavery, giving to such State, pecuniary aid, to be used by such State in its discretion, to compensate for the inconveniences, public and private, produced by such change of System."

It was high time, he thought, that the idea of a gradual, compensated Emancipation, should begin to occupy the minds of those interested, "so that," to use his own words, "they may begin to consider whether to accept or reject it," should Congress approve the suggestion.

Congress did approve, and adopt, the Joint-Resolution, as we know—despite the opposition from the loyal element of the Border States—an opposition made in the teeth of their concession that Mr. Lincoln, in recommending its adoption, was "solely moved by a high patriotism and sincere devotion to the glory of his Country."

But, consistently with their usual course, they went to the House of Representatives, fresh from the Presidential presence, and, with their ears still ringing with the common-sense utterances of the President, half of them voted against the Resolution, while the other half refrained from voting at all. And their opposition to this wise and moderate proposition was mainly based upon the idea that it carried with it a threat—a covert threat.

It certainly was a warning, taking it in connection with the balance of the Message, but a very wise and timely one.

These loyal Border-State men, however, could not see its wisdom, and at a full meeting held upon the subject decided to oppose it, as they afterward did. Its conciliatory spirit they could not comprehend; the kindly, temperate warning, they would not heed. The most moderate of them all,—[Mr. Crittenden of Kentucky.]—in the most moderate of his utterances, could not bring himself to the belief that this Resolution was "a measure exactly suited to the times."

[And such was the fatuity existing among the Slave-holders of the Border States, that not one of those Slave States had wisdom enough to take the liberal offer thus made by the General Government, of compensation. They afterward found their Slaves freed without compensation.]

So, also, one month later, (April 11, 1862), when the Senate Bill proposing Emancipation in the District of Columbia, was before the House, the same spokesman and leader of the loyal Border-State men opposed it strenuously as not being suited to the times. For, he persuasively protested: "I do not say that you have not the power; but would not that power be, at such a time as this, most unwisely and indiscreetly exercised. That is the point. Of all the times when an attempt was ever made to carry this measure, is not this the most inauspicious? Is it not a time when the measure is most likely to produce danger and mischief to the Country at large? So it seems to me."

It was not now, nor would it ever be, the time, to pass this, or any other measure, touching the Institution of Slavery, likely to benefit that Union to which these men professed such love and loyalty.

Their opposition, however, to the march of events, was of little avail—even when backed, as was almost invariably the case, by the other Democratic votes from the Free States. The opposition was obstructive, but not effectual. For this reason it was perhaps the more irritating to the Republicans, who were anxious to put Slavery where their great leader, Mr. Lincoln, had long before said it should be placed—"in course of ultimate extinction."

This very irritation, however, only served to press such Anti-Slavery Measures more rapidly forward. By the 19th of June, 1862, a Bill "to secure Freedom to all persons within the Territories of the United States"—after a more strenuous fight against it than ever, on the part of Loyal and Copperhead Democrats, both from the Border and Free States,—had passed Congress, and been approved by President Lincoln. It provided, in just so many words, "That, from and after the passage of this Act, there shall be neither Slavery nor involuntary servitude in any of the Territories of the United States now existing, or which may at any time hereafter be formed or acquired by the United States, otherwise than in punishment of crime, whereof the party shall have been duly convicted."

Here, then, at last, was the great end and aim, with which Mr. Lincoln and the Republican Party started out, accomplished. To repeat his phrase, Slavery was certainly now in course of ultimate extinction.

But since that doctrine had been first enunciated by Mr. Lincoln, events had changed the aspect of things. War had broken out, and the Slaves of those engaged in armed Rebellion against the authority of the United States Government, had been actually employed, as we have seen, on Rebel works and fortifications whose guns were trailed upon the Armies of the Union.

And now, the question of Slavery had ceased to be simply whether it should be put in course of ultimate extinction, but whether, as a War Measure—as a means of weakening the Enemy and strengthening the Union—the time had not already come to extinguish it, so far, at least, as the Slaves of those participating in the Rebellion, were concerned.

Congress, as has been heretofore noted, had already long and heatedly debated various propositions referring to Slavery and African Colonization, and had enacted such of them as, in its wisdom, were considered necessary; and was now entering a further stormy period of contention upon various other projects touching the Abolition of the Fugitive Slave Laws, the Confiscation of Rebel Property, and the Emancipation of Slaves—all of which, of course, had been, and would be, vehemently assailed by the loyal Border-States men and their Free-State Democratic allies.

This contention proceeded largely upon the lines of construction of that clause in the Constitution of the United States and its Amendments, which provides that no person shall be deprived of Life, Liberty, or Property, without due process of Law, etc. The one side holding that, since the beginning of our Government, Slaves had been, under this clause, Unconstitutionally deprived of their Liberty; the other side holding that Slaves being "property," it would be Unconstitutional under the same clause, to deprive the Slave-owner of his Slave property.

Mr. Crittenden, the leader of the loyal Border-States men in Congress, was at this time especially eloquent on this latter view of the Constitution. In his speech of April 23, 1862, in the House of Representatives, he even undertook to defend American Slavery under the shield of English Liberty! Said he: "It is necessary for the prosperity of any Government, for peace and harmony, that every man who acquires property shall feel that he shall be protected in the enjoyment of it, and in his right to hold it. It elevates the man; it gives him a feeling of dignity. It is the great old English doctrine of Liberty. Said Lord Mansfield, the rain may beat against the cabin of an Englishman, the snow may penetrate it, but the King dare not enter it without the consent of its owner. That is the true English spirit. It is the source of England's power."

And again: "The idea of property is deeply seated in our minds. By the English Law and by the American Law you have the right to take the life of any man who attempts, by violence, to take your property from you. So far does the Spirit of these Laws go. Let us not break down this idea of property. It is the animating spirit of the Country. Indeed it is the Spirit of Liberty and Freedom."

There was at this time, a growing belief in the minds of these loyal Border-States men, that this question of Slavery-abolition was reaching a crisis. They saw "the handwriting on the wall," but left no stone unturned to prevent, or at least to avert for a time, the coming catastrophe. They egged Congress, in the language of the distinguished Kentuckian, to "Let these unnecessary measures alone, for the present;" and, as to the President, they now, not only volunteered in his defense, against the attacks of others, but strove also to capture him by their arch flatteries.

"Sir,"—said Mr. Crittenden, in one of his most eloquent bursts, in the House of Representatives,—"it is not my duty, perhaps, to defend the President of the United States. * * * I voted against Mr. Lincoln, and opposed him honestly and sincerely; but Mr. Lincoln has won me to his side. There is a niche in the Temple of Fame, a niche near to Washington, which should be occupied by the statue of him who shall, save this Country. Mr. Lincoln has a mighty destiny. It is for him, if he will, to step into that niche. It is for him to be but President of the People of the United States, and there will his statue be. But, if he choose to be, in these times, a mere sectarian and a party man, that niche will be reserved for some future and better Patriot. It is in his power to occupy a place next Washington,—the Founder, and the Preserver, side by side. Sir, Mr. Lincoln is no coward. His not doing what the Constitution forbade him to do, is no proof of his cowardice."

On the other hand, Owen Lovejoy, the fiery Abolitionist, the very next day after the above remarks of Mr. Crittenden were delivered in the House, made a great speech in reply, taking the position that "either Slavery, or the Republic, must perish; and the question for us to decide is, which shall it be?"

He declared to the House: "You cannot put down the rebellion and restore the Union, without destroying Slavery." He quoted the sublime language of Curran touching the Spirit of the British Law, which consecrates the soil of Britain to the genius of Universal Emancipation,

[In these words:

"I speak in the Spirit of the British law, which makes Liberty commensurate with, and inseparable from, the British soil; which proclaims even to the stranger and the sojourner the moment he sets his foot upon British earth, that the ground on which he treads is holy, and consecrated by the genius Of UNIVERSAL EMANCIPATION.

"No matter in what language his doom may have been pronounced; no matter what complexion incompatible with Freedom, an Indian or an

African sun may have burnt upon him; no matter in what disastrous battle his Liberty may have been cloven down; no matter with what solemnities he may have been devoted upon the altar of Slavery; the first moment he touches the sacred soil of Britain, the altar and the god sink together in the dust; his Soul walks abroad in her own majesty; his Body swells beyond the measure of his chains, that burst from around him, and he stands redeemed, regenerated, and disenthralled by the irresistible genius of UNIVERSAL EMANCIPATION."]

And Cowper's verse, wherein the poet says:

"Slaves cannot breathe in England; if their lungs Receive our air, that moment they are Free,"

—and, after expressing his solicitude to have this true of America, as it already was true of the District of Columbia, he proceeded to say:

"The gentleman from Kentucky says he has a niche for Abraham Lincoln. Where is it? He pointed upward! But, Sir, should the President follow the counsels of that gentleman, and become the defender and perpetuator of human Slavery, he should point downward to some dungeon in the Temple of Moloch, who feeds on human blood and is surrounded with fires, where are forged manacles and chains for human limbs—in the crypts and recesses of whose Temple, woman is scourged, and man tortured, and outside whose walls are lying dogs, gorged with human flesh, as Byron describes them stretched around Stamboul. That is a suitable place for the statue of one who would defend and perpetuate human Slavery."

And then—after saying that "the friends of American Slavery need not beslime the President with their praise. He is an Anti-Slavery man. He hates human Bondage "—the orator added these glowing words:

"I, too, have a niche for Abraham Lincoln; but it is in Freedom's Holy Fane, and not in the blood-besmeared Temple of human Bondage; not surrounded by Slaves, fetters and chains, but with the symbols of Freedom; not dark with Bondage, but radiant with the light of Liberty. In that niche he shall stand proudly, nobly, gloriously, with shattered fetters and broken chains and slave-whips beneath his feet. If Abraham Lincoln pursues the path, evidently pointed out for him in the providence of God, as I believe he will, then he will occupy the proud position I have indicated. That is a fame worth living for; ay, more, that is a fame worth dying for, though that death led through the blood of Gethsemane and the agony of the Accursed Tree. That is a fame which has glory and honor and immortality and Eternal Life. Let Abraham Lincoln make himself, as I trust he will, the Emancipator, the Liberator, as he has the opportunity of doing, and his name shall not only be enrolled in this Earthly Temple, but it will be traced on the living stones of that Temple which rears itself amid the Thrones and Hierarchies of Heaven, whose top-stone is to be brought in with shouting of 'Grace, grace unto it!'"

We have seen how the loyal Border-State men, through their chosen Representative—finding that their steady and unfaltering opposition to all Mr. Lincoln's propositions, while quite ineffectual, did not serve by any means to increase his respect for their peculiar kind of loyalty —offered him posthumous honors and worship if he would but do as they desired. Had they possessed the power, no doubt they would have taken him up into an exceeding high mountain and have offered to him all the Kingdoms of the Earth to do their bidding. But their temptations were of no avail.

President Lincoln's duty, and inclination alike—no less than the earnest importunities of the Abolitionists—carried him in the opposite direction; but carried him no farther than he thought it safe, and wise, to go. For, in whatever he might do on this burning question of Emancipation, he was determined to secure that adequate support from the People without which even Presidential Proclamations are waste paper.

But now, May 9, 1862, was suddenly issued by General Hunter, commanding the "Department of the South," comprising Georgia, Florida and South Carolina, his celebrated Order announcing Martial Law, in those States, as a Military Necessity, and—as "Slavery and Martial Law in a Free Country are altogether incompatible"—declaring all Slaves therein, "forever Free."

This second edition, as it were, of Fremont's performance, at once threw the loyal Border-State men into a terrible ferment. Again, they, and their Copperhead and other Democratic friends of the North, meanly professed belief that this was but a part of Mr. Lincoln's programme, and that his apparent backwardness was the cloak to hide his Anti-Slavery aggressiveness and insincerity.

How hurtful the insinuations, and even direct charges, of the day, made by these men against President Lincoln, must have been to his honest, sincere, and sensitive nature, can scarcely be conceived by those who did not know him; while, on the other hand, the reckless impatience of some of his friends for "immediate and universal Emancipation," and their complaints at his slow progress toward that goal of their hopes, must have been equally trying.

True to himself, however, and to the wise conservative course which he had marked out, and, thus far, followed, President Lincoln hastened to disavow Hunter's action in the premises, by a Proclamation, heretofore given, declaring that no person had been authorized by the United States Government to declare the Slaves of any State, Free; that Hunter's action in this respect was void; that, as Commander-in-chief he reserved solely to himself, the questions, first, as to whether he had the power to declare the Slaves of any State or States, Free, and, second, whether the time and necessity for the exercise of such supposed power had arrived. And then, as we may remember, he proceeded to cite the adoption, by overwhelming majorities in Congress, of the Joint Resolution offering pecuniary aid from the National Government to "any State which may adopt a gradual abolishment of Slavery;" and to make a most earnest appeal, for support, to the Border-States and to their people, as being "the most interested in the subject matter."

In his Special Message to Congress,—[Of March 6, 1862.]—recommending the passage of that Joint Resolution, he had plainly and emphatically declared himself against sudden Emancipation of Slaves. He had therein distinctly said: "In my judgment, gradual, and not immediate, Emancipation, is better for all." And now, in this second appeal of his to the Border-States men, to patriotically close with the proposal embraced in that. Resolution, he said: "The changes it contemplates would come gently as the dews of Heaven, not rending or wrecking anything. Will you not embrace it? So much good has not been done, by one effort, in all past time, as, in the providence of God, it is now your high privilege to do! May the vast future not have to lament that you have neglected it!"

[The following letter, from Sumner, shows the impatience of some of the President's friends, the confidence he inspired in others nearer in his counsels, and how entirely, at this time, his mind was absorbed in his project for gradual and compensated Emancipation.]

"SENATE CHAMBER, June 5, 1862.

"MY DEAR SIR.—Your criticism of the President is hasty. I am confident that, if you knew him as I do, you would not make it. Of course the President cannot be held responsible for the misfeasances of subordinates, unless adopted or at least tolerated by him. And I am sure that nothing unjust or ungenerous will be tolerated, much less adopted, by him.

"I am happy to let you know that he has no sympathy with Stanly in his absurd wickedness, closing the schools, nor again in his other act of turning our camp into a hunting ground for Slaves. He repudiates both—positively. The latter point has occupied much of his thought; and the newspapers have not gone too far in recording his repeated declarations, which I have often heard from his own lips, that Slaves finding their way into the National lines are never to be Re-enslaved—This is his conviction, expressed without reserve.

"Could you have seen the President—as it was my privilege often—while he was considering the great questions on which he has already acted—the invitation to Emancipation in the States, Emancipation in the District of Columbia, and the acknowledgment of the Independence of Hayti and Liberia—even your zeal would have been satisfied, for you would have felt the sincerity of his purpose to do what he could to carry forward the principles of the Declaration of Independence.

"His whole soul was occupied, especially by the first proposition, which was peculiarly his own. In familiar intercourse with him, I remember nothing more touching than the earnestness and completeness with which he embraced this idea. To his mind, it was just and beneficent, while it promised the sure end of Slavery. Of course, to me, who had already proposed a bridge of gold for the retreating fiend, it was most welcome. Proceeding from the President, it must take its place among the great events of history.

"If you are disposed to be impatient at any seeming shortcomings, think, I pray you, of what has been done in a brief period, and from the past discern the sure promise of the future. Knowing something of my convictions and of the ardor with which I maintain them, you may, perhaps, derive some assurance from my confidence; I may say to you, therefore, stand by the Administration. If need be, help it by word and act, but stand by it and have faith in it.

"I wish that you really knew the President, and had heard the artless expression of his convictions on those questions which concern you so deeply. You might, perhaps, wish that he were less cautious, but you would be grateful that he is so true to all that you have at heart. Believe me, therefore, you are wrong, and I regret it the more because of my desire to see all our friends stand firmly together.

"If I write strongly it is because I feel strongly; for my constant and intimate intercourse with the President, beginning with the 4th of March, not only binds me peculiarly to his Administration, but gives me a personal as well as a political interest in seeing that justice is done him.

"Believe me, my dear Sir, with much regard, ever faithfully yours,

"CHARLES SUMNER."

But stones are not more deaf to entreaty than were the ears of the loyal Border-State men and their allies to President Lincoln's renewed appeal. "Ephraim" was "wedded to his idols."

McClellan too—immediately after his retreat from the Chickahominy to the James River—seized the opportunity afforded by the disasters to our arms, for which he was responsible, to write to President Lincoln a letter (dated July 7, 1862) in which he admonished him that owing to the "critical" condition of the Army of the Potomac, and the danger of its being "overwhelmed" by the Enemy in front, the President must now substantially assume and exercise the powers of a Dictator, or all would be lost; that "neither Confiscation of property * * * nor forcible Abolition of Slavery, should be contemplated for a moment;" and that "A declaration of Radical views, especially upon Slavery, will rapidly disintegrate our present Armies."

Harried, and worried, on all sides,—threatened even by the Commander of the Army of the Potomac,—it is not surprising, in view of the apparently irreconcilable attitude of the loyal Border-State men to gradual and compensated Emancipation, that the tension of President Lincoln's mind began to feel a measure of relief in contemplating Military Emancipation in the teeth of all such threats.

He had long since made up his mind that the existence of Slavery was not compatible with the preservation of the Union. The only question now was, how to get rid of it? If the worst should come to the worst—despite McClellan's threat—he would have to risk everything on the turn of the die—would have to "play his last card;" and that "last card" was Military Emancipation. Yet still he disliked to play it. The time and necessity for it had not yet arrived—although he thought he saw them coming.

[In the course of an article in the New York Tribune, August, 1885, Hon. George S. Boutwell tells of an interview in "July or early in August" of 1862, with President Lincoln, at which the latter read two letters: one from a Louisiana man "who claimed to be a Union man," but sought to impress the President with "the dangers and evils of Emancipation;" the other, Mr. Lincoln's reply to him, in which, says Mr. B., "he used this expression: 'you must not expect me to give up this Government without playing my last card.' Emancipation was his last card."]

Things were certainly, at this time, sufficiently unpromising to chill the sturdiest Patriot's heart. It is true, we had scored some important victories in the West; but in the East, our arms seemed fated to disaster after disaster. Belmont, Fort Henry, Fort Donelson, and Pittsburg Landing, were names whose mention made the blood of Patriots to surge in their veins; and Corinth, too, had fallen. But in the East, McClellan's profitless campaign against Richmond, and especially his disastrous "change of base" by a "masterly" seven days' retreat, involving as many bloody battles, had greatly dispirited all Union men, and encouraged the Rebels and Rebel-sympathizers to renewed hopes and efforts.

And, as reverses came to the Union Arms, so seemed to grow proportionately the efforts, on all sides, to force forward, or to stave off, as the case might be, the great question of the liberation and arming of the Slaves, as a War Measure, under the War powers of the Constitution. It was about this time (July 12, 1862) that President Lincoln determined to make a third, and last, attempt to avert the necessity for thus emancipating and arming the Slaves. He invited all the Senators and Representatives in Congress from the Border-States, to an interview at the White House, and made to them the appeal, heretofore in these pages given at length.

It was an earnest, eloquent, wise, kindly, patriotic, fatherly appeal in behalf of his old proposition, for a gradual, compensated Emancipation, by the Slave States, aided by the resources of the National Government.

At the very time of making it, he probably had, in his drawer, the rough draft of the Proclamation which was soon to give Liberty to all the Colored millions of the Land.

[McPherson gives a letter, written from Washington, by Owen Lovejoy

(Feb. 22, 1864), to Wm. Lloyd Garrison, in which the following passage occurs:

"Recurring to the President, there are a great many reports concerning him which seem to be reliable and authentic, which, after all, are not so. It was currently reported among the Anti-Slavery men of Illinois that the Emancipation Proclamation was extorted from him by the outward pressure, and particularly by the Delegation from the Christian Convention that met at Chicago.

"Now, the fact is this, as I had it from his own lips: He had written the Proclamation in the Summer, as early as June, I think—but will not be certain as to the precise time—and called his Cabinet together, and informed them he had written it and meant to make it, but wanted to read it to them for any criticism or remarks as to its features or details.

"After having done so, Mr. Seward suggested whether it would not be well for him to withhold its publication until after we had gained some substantial advantage in the Field, as at that time we had met with many reverses, and it might be considered a cry of despair. He told me he thought the suggestion a wise one, and so held on to the Proclamation until after the Battle of Antietam."]

Be that as it may, however, sufficient evidences exist, to prove that he must have been fully aware, at the time of making that appeal to the supposed patriotism of these Border-State men, how much, how very much, depended on the manner of their reception of it.

To him, that meeting was a very solemn and portentous one. He had studied the question long and deeply—not from the standpoint of his own mere individual feelings and judgment, but from that of fair Constitutional construction, as interpreted by the light of Natural or General Law and right reason. What he sought to impress upon them was, that an immediate decision by the Border-States to adopt, and in due time carry out, with the financial help of the General Government, a policy of gradual Emancipation, would simultaneously solve the two intimately-blended problems of Slavery-destruction and Union-preservation, in the best possible manner for the pockets and feelings of the Border-State Slave-holder, and for the other interests of both Border-State Slave-holder and Slave.

His great anxiety was to "perpetuate," as well as to save, to the People of the World, the imperiled form of Popular Government, and assure to it a happy and a grand future.

He begged these Congressmen from the Border-States, to help him carry out this, his beneficent plan, in the way that was best for all, and thus at the same time utterly deprive the Rebel Confederacy of that hope, which still possessed them, of ultimately gathering these States into their rebellious fold. And he very plainly, at the same time, confessed that he desired this relief from the Abolition pressure upon him, which had been growing more intense ever since he had repudiated the Hunter proclamation.

But the President's earnest appeal to these loyal Representatives in Congress from the Border-States, was, as we have seen, in vain. It might as well have been made to actual Rebels, for all the good it did. For, a few days afterward, they sent to him a reply signed by more than two-thirds of those present, hitherto given at length in these pages, in which-after loftily sneering at the proposition as "an interference by this Government with a question which peculiarly and exclusively belonged to" their "respective States, on which they had not sought advice or solicited aid," throwing doubts upon the Constitutional power of the General Government to give the financial aid, and undertaking by statistics to prove that it would absolutely bankrupt the Government to give such aid,—they insultingly declared, in substance, that they could not "trust anything to the contingencies of future legislation," and that Congress must "provide sufficient funds" and place those funds in the President's hands for the purpose, before the Border-States and their people would condescend even to "take this proposition into careful consideration, for such decision as in their judgment is demanded by their interest, their honor, and their duty to the whole Country."

Very different in tone, to be sure, was the minority reply, which, after stating that "the leaders of the Southern Rebellion have offered to abolish Slavery among them as a condition to Foreign Intervention in favor of their Independence as a Nation," concluded with the terse and loyal deduction: "If they can give up Slavery to destroy the Union, we can surely ask our people to consider the question of Emancipation to save the Union."

But those who signed this latter reply were few, among the many. Practically, the Border-State men were a unit against Mr. Lincoln's proposition, and against its fair consideration by their people. He asked for meat, and they gave him a stone.

Only a few days before this interview, President Lincoln—alarmed by the report of McClellan, that the magnificent Army of the Potomac under his command, which, only three months before, had boasted 161,000 men, had dwindled down to not more than "50,000 men left with their colors"—had been to the front, at Harrison's Landing, on the James river, and, although he had not found things quite so disheartening as he had been led to believe, yet they were bad enough, for only 86,000 men were found by him on duty, while 75,000 were unaccounted for—of which number 34,4172 were afterward reported as "absent by authority."

This condition of affairs, in connection with the fact that McClellan was always calling for more troops, undoubtedly had its influence in bringing Mr. Lincoln's mind to the conviction, hitherto mentioned, of the fast-approaching Military necessity for Freeing and Arming the Slaves.

It was to ward this off, if possible, that he had met and appealed to the Border-State Representatives. They had answered him with sneers and insults; and nothing was left him but the extreme course of almost immediate Emancipation.

Long and anxiously he had thought over the matter, but the time for action was at hand.

And now, it cannot be better told, than in President Lincoln's own words, as given to the portrait-painter Carpenter, and recorded in the latter's, "Six months in the White House," what followed:

"It had got to be," said he, "midsummer, 1862. Things had gone on from bad to worse, until I felt that we had reached the end of our rope on the plan of operations we had been pursuing; that we had about played our last card, and must change our tactics, or lose the game!

"I now determined upon the adoption of the Emancipation Policy; and, without consultation with, or the knowledge of, the Cabinet, I prepared the original draft of the Proclamation, and, after much anxious thought, called a Cabinet meeting upon the subject. This was the last of July, or the first part of the month of August, 1862." (The exact date he did not remember.)

"This Cabinet meeting took place, I think, upon a Saturday. All were present, excepting Mr. Blair, the Postmaster-General, who was absent at the opening of the discussion, but came in subsequently. I said to the Cabinet, that I had resolved upon this step, and had not called them together to ask their advice, but to lay the subject-matter of a Proclamation before them; suggestions as to which would be in order, after they had heard it read.

"Mr. Lovejoy was in error" when he stated "that it excited no comment, excepting on the part of Secretary Seward. Various suggestions were offered. Secretary Chase wished the language stronger, in reference to the arming of the Blacks. Mr. Blair, after he came in, deprecated the policy, on the ground that it would cost the Administration the fall elections.

"Nothing, however, was offered, that I had not already fully anticipated and settled in my own mind, until Secretary Seward spoke. He said in substance: 'Mr. President, I approve of the Proclamation, but I question the expediency of its issue at this juncture. The depression of the public mind, consequent upon our repeated reverses, is so great that I fear the effect of so important a step. It may be viewed as the last Measure of an exhausted Government, a cry for help, the Government stretching forth its hands to Ethiopia, instead of Ethiopia stretching forth her hands to the Government.'

"His idea," said the President "was that it would be considered our last shriek, on the retreat." (This was his precise expression.) "' Now,' continued Mr. Seward, 'while I approve the Measure, I suggest, Sir, that you postpone its issue, until you can give it to the Country supported by Military success, instead of issuing it, as would be the case now, upon the greatest disasters of the War!'"

Mr. Lincoln continued: "The wisdom of the view of the Secretary of State, struck me with very great force. It was an aspect of the case that, in all my thought upon the subject, I had entirely overlooked. The result was that I put the draft of the Proclamation aside, as you do your sketch for a picture, waiting for a victory."

It may not be amiss to interrupt the President's narration to Mr. Carpenter, at this point, with a few words touching "the Military Situation."

After McClellan's inexplicable retreat from before the Rebel Capital—when, having gained a great victory at Malvern Hills, Richmond would undoubtedly have been ours, had he but followed it up, instead of ordering his victorious troops to retreat like "a whipped Army"—[See General Hooker's testimony before the Committee on the Conduct of the War.]— his recommendation, in the extraordinary letter (of July 7th) to the President, for the creation of the office of General-in-Chief, was adopted, and Halleck, then at Corinth, was ordered East, to fill it.

Pope had previously been called from the West, to take command of the troops covering Washington, comprising some 40,000 men, known as the Army of Virginia; and, finding cordial cooperation with McClellan impossible, had made a similar suggestion.

Soon after Halleck's arrival, that General ordered the transfer of the Army of the Potomac, from Harrison's Landing to Acquia creek—on the Potomac—with a view to a new advance upon Richmond, from the Rappahannock river.

While this was being slowly accomplished, Lee, relieved from fears for Richmond, decided to advance upon Washington, and speedily commenced the movement.

On the 8th of August, 1862, Stonewall Jackson, leading the Rebel advance, had crossed the Rapidan; on the 9th the bloody Battle of Cedar Mountain had been fought with part of Pope's Army; and on the 11th, Jackson had retreated across the Rapidan again.

Subsequently, Pope having retired across the Rappahannock, Lee's Forces, by flanking Pope's Army, again resumed their Northern advance. August 28th and 29th witnessed the bloody Battles of Groveton and Gainesville, Virginia; the 30th saw the defeat of Pope, by Lee, at the second great Battle of Bull Run, and the falling back of Pope's Army toward Washington; and the succeeding Battle of Chantilly took place September 1, 1862.

It is not necessary at this time to even touch upon the causes and agencies which brought such misfortune to the Union Arms, under Pope. It is sufficient to say here, that the disaster of the second Bull Run was a dreadful blow to the Union Cause, and correspondingly elated the Rebels.

Jefferson Davis, in transmitting to the Rebel Congress at Richmond, Lee's victorious announcements, said, in his message: "From these dispatches it will be seen that God has again extended His shield over our patriotic Army, and has blessed the cause of the Confederacy with a second signal victory, on the field already memorable by the gallant achievement of our troops."

Flushed with victory, but wisely avoiding the fortifications of the National Capital, Lee's Forces now swept past Washington; crossed the Potomac, near Point of Rocks, at its rear; and menaced both the National Capital and Baltimore.

Yielding to the apparent necessity of the moment, the President again placed. McClellan in command of the Armies about Washington, to wit: the Army of the Potomac; Burnside's troops that had come up from North Carolina; what remained of Pope's Army of Virginia; and the large reinforcements from fresh levies, constantly and rapidly pouring in.

[This was probably about the time of the occurrence of an amusing incident, touching Lincoln, McClellan, and the fortifications around Washington, afterward told by General J. G. Barnard, then Chief of Engineers on the staff of General George B. McClellan.—See New York Tribune, October 21, 1885. It seems that the fortifications having been completed, McClellan invited Mr. Lincoln and his Cabinet to inspect them. "On the day appointed," said Barnard, "the Inspection commenced at Arlington, to the Southwest of Washington, and in front of the Enemy. We followed the line of the works southerly, and recrossed the Potomac to the easterly side of the river, and continued along the line easterly of Washington and into the heaviest of all the fortifications on the northerly side of Washington. When we reached this point the President asked General McClellan to explain the necessity of so strong a fortification between Washington and the North.

"General McClellan replied: 'Why, Mr. President, according to Military Science it is our duty to guard against every possible or supposable contingency that may arise. For example, if under any circumstances, however fortuitous, the Enemy, by any chance or freak, should, in a last resort, get in behind Washington, in his efforts to capture the city, why, there the fort is to defend it.'

"'Yes, that's so General,' said the President; 'the precaution is doubtless a wise one, and I'm glad to get so clear an explanation, for it reminds me of an interesting question once discussed for several weeks in our Lyceum, or Moot Court, at Springfield, Ill., soon after I began reading law.'

"'Ah!' says General McClellan. 'What question was that, Mr. President?'

"'The question,' Mr. Lincoln replied, 'was, "Why does man have breasts?"'" and he added that after many evenings' debate, the question was submitted to the presiding Judge, who wisely decided 'That if under any circumstances, however fortuitous, or by any chance or freak, no matter of what nature or by what cause, a man should have a baby, there would be the breasts to nurse it.'"]

Yet, it was not until the 17th of September that the Battle of Antietam was fought, and Lee defeated—and then only to be allowed to slip back, across the Potomac, on the 18th—McClellan leisurely following him, across that river, on the 2nd of November!

[Arnold, in his "Life of Abraham Lincoln," says that President Lincoln said of him: "With all his failings as a soldier, McClellan is a pleasant and scholarly gentleman. He is an admirable Engineer, but" he added, "he seems to have a special talent for a stationary Engine."]

On the 5th, McClellan was relieved,—Burnside taking the command,—and Union men breathed more freely again.

But to return to the subject of Emancipation. President Lincoln's own words have already been given—in conversation with Carpenter—down to the reading of the Proclamation to his Cabinet, and Seward's suggestion to "wait for a victory" before issuing it, and how, adopting that advice, he laid the Proclamation aside, waiting for a victory.

"From time to time," said Mr. Lincoln, continuing his narration, "I added or changed a line, touching it up here and there, anxiously waiting the progress of events. Well, the next news we had was of Pope's disaster at Bull Run. Things looked darker than ever. Finally, came the week of the Battle of Antietam. I determined to wait no longer.

"The news came, I think, on Wednesday, that the advantage was on our side. I was then staying at the Soldiers' Home (three miles out of Washington.) Here I finished writing the second draft of the preliminary Proclamation; came up on Saturday; called the Cabinet together to hear it; and it was published the following Monday."

It is not uninteresting to note, in this connection, upon the same authority, that at the final meeting of the Cabinet prior to this issue of the Proclamation, when the third paragraph was read, and the words of the draft "will recognize the Freedom of such Persons," were reached, Mr. Seward suggested the insertion of the words "and maintain" after the word "recognize;" and upon his insistence, the President said, "the words finally went in."

At last, then, had gone forth the Fiat—telegraphed and read throughout the Land, on that memorable 22d of September, 1862—which, with the supplemental Proclamation of January 1, 1863, was to bring joy and Freedom to the millions of Black Bondsmen of the South.

Just one month before its issue, in answer to Horace Greeley's Open letter berating him for "the seeming subserviency" of his "policy to the Slave-holding, Slave up-holding interest," etc., President Lincoln had written his famous "Union letter" in which he had conservatively said: "My paramount object is to save the Union, and not either to save or destroy Slavery. If I could save the Union without freeing any Slave, I would do it—and if I could save it by freeing all the Slaves, I would do it—and if I could save it by freeing some, and leaving others alone, I would also do that."

No one outside of his Cabinet dreamed, at the time he made that answer, that the Proclamation of Emancipation was already written, and simply awaited a turn in the tide of battle for its issue!

Still less could it have been supposed, when, on the 13th of September—only two days before Stonewall Jackson had invested, attacked, and captured Harper's Ferry with nearly 12,000 prisoners, 73 cannon, and 13,000 small arms, besides other spoils of War—Mr. Lincoln received the deputation from the religious bodies of Chicago, bearing a Memorial for the immediate issue of such a Proclamation.

The very language of his reply,—where he said to them: "It is my earnest desire to know the will of Providence in this matter. And if I can learn what it is, I will do it! These are not, however, the days of miracles, and I suppose it will be granted that I am not to expect a direct revelation. I must study the plain physical aspects of the case, ascertain what is possible, and learn what appears to be wise and right"—when taken in connection with the very strong argument with which he followed it up, against the policy of Emancipation advocated in the Memorial, and his intimation that a Proclamation of Emancipation issued by him "must necessarily be inoperative, like the Pope's Bull against the Comet!"—would almost seem to have been adopted with the very object of veiling his real purpose from the public eye, and leaving the public mind in doubt. At all events, it had that effect.

Arnold, in his "Life of Lincoln," says of this time, when General Lee was marching Northward toward Pennsylvania, that "now, the President, with that tinge of superstition which ran through his character, 'made,' as he said, 'a solemn vow to God, that, if Lee was driven back, he would issue the Proclamation;'" and, in the light of that statement, the concluding words of Mr. Lincoln's reply to the deputation aforesaid:—"I can assure you that the subject is on my mind, by day and night, more than any other. Whatever shall appear to be God's will, I will do,"—have a new meaning.

The Emancipation Proclamation, when issued, was a great surprise, but was none the less generally well-received by the Union Armies, and throughout the Loyal States of the Union, while, in some of them, its reception was most enthusiastic.

It happened, too, as we have seen, that the Convention of the Governors of the Loyal States met at Altoona, Penn., on the very day of its promulgation, and in an address to the President adopted by these loyal Governors, they publicly hailed it "with heartfelt gratitude and encouraged hope," and declared that "the decision of the President to strike at the root of the Rebellion will lend new vigor to efforts, and new life and hope to the hearts, of the People."

On the other hand, the loyal Border-States men were dreadfully exercised on the subject; and those of them in the House of Representatives emphasized their disapproval by their votes, when, on the 11th and 15th of the following December, Resolutions, respectively denouncing, and endorsing, "the policy of Emancipation, as indicated in that Proclamation," of September 22, 1862, were offered and voted on.

In spite of the loyal Border-States men's bitter opposition, however, the Resolution endorsing that policy as a War Measure, and declaring the Proclamation to be "an exercise of power with proper regard for the rights of the States and the perpetuity of Free Government," as we have seen, passed the House.

Of course the Rebels themselves, against whom it was aimed, gnashed their teeth in impotent rage over the Proclamation. But they lost no time in declaring that it was only a proof of what they had always announced: that the War was not for the preservation of the American Union, but for the destruction of African Slavery, and the spoilation of the Southern States.

Through their friends and emissaries, in the Border and other Loyal States of the Union,—the "Knights of the Golden Circle,"—

[The "Knights of the Golden Circle" was the most extensive of these Rebel organizations. It was "an auxiliary force to the Rebel Army." Its members took an obligation of the most binding character, the violation of which was punishable by death, which obligation, in the language of another, "pledged them to use every possible means in their power to aid the Rebels to gain their Independence; to aid and assist Rebel prisoners to escape; to vote for no one for Office who was not opposed to the further prosecution of the War; to encourage desertions from the Union Army; to protect the Rebels in all things necessary to carry out their designs, even to the burning and destroying of towns and cities, if necessary to produce the desired result; to give such information as they had, at all times, of the movements of our Armies, and of the return of soldiers to their homes; and to try and prevent their going back to their regiments at the front."

In other words the duty of the Organization and of its members, was to hamper, oppose, and prevent all things possible that were being done at any time for the Union Cause, and to encourage, forward, and help all things possible in behalf of the Rebel Cause.

It was to be a flanking force of the Enemy—a reverse fire—a fire in the rear of the Union Army, by Northern men; a powerful cooperating force— all the more powerful because secret—operating safely because secretly and in silence—and breeding discontent, envy, hatred, and other ill feelings wherever possible, in and out of Army circles, from the highest to the lowest, at all possible times, and on all possible occasions.]

—the "Order of American Knights" or "Sons of Liberty," and other Copperhead organizations, tainted with more or less of Treason—they stirred up all the old dregs of Pro-Slavery feeling that could possibly he reached; but while the venomous acts and utterances of such organizations, and the increased and vindictive energy of the armed Rebels themselves, had a tendency to disquiet the public mind with apprehensions as to the result of the Proclamation, and whether, indeed, Mr. Lincoln himself would be able to resist the pressure, and stand up to his promise of that Supplemental Proclamation which would give definiteness and practical effect to the preliminary one, the masses of the people of the Loyal States had faith in him.

There was also another element, in chains, at the South, which at this time must have been trembling with that mysterious hope of coming Emancipation for their Race, conveyed so well in Whittier's lines, commencing: "We pray de Lord; he gib us signs, dat some day we be Free" —a hope which had long animated them, as of something almost too good for them to live to enjoy, but which, as the War progressed, appeared to grow nearer and nearer, until now they seemed to see the promised Land, flowing with milk and honey, its beautiful hills and vales smiling under the quickening beams of Freedom's glorious sun. But ah! should they enter there?—or must they turn away again into the old wilderness of their Slavery, and this blessed Liberty, almost within their grasp, mockingly elude them?

They had not long to wait for an answer. The 1st of January, 1863, arrived, and with it—as a precious New Year's Gift—came the Supplemental Proclamation, bearing the sacred boon of Liberty to the Emancipated millions.

At last, at last, no American need blush to stand up and proclaim his land indeed, and in truth, "the Land of Freedom."

THE ARMED NEGRO

Little over five months had passed, since the occurrence of the great event in the history of the American Nation mentioned in the preceding Chapter, before the Freed Negro, now bearing arms in defense of the Union and of his own Freedom, demonstrated at the first attack on Port Hudson the wisdom of emancipating and arming the Slave, as a War measure. He seemed thoroughly to appreciate and enter into the spirit of the words; "who would be Free, himself must strike the blow."

At the attack (of May 27th, 1863), on Port Hudson, where it held the right, the "Black Brigade" covered itself with glory.

At Baton Rouge, before starting for Port Hudson, the color-guard of the First Louisiana Regiment—of the Black Brigade—received the Regimental flags from their white colonel, (Col. Stafford,) then under arrest, in a speech which ended with the injunction: "Color-guard, protect, defend, die for, but do not surrender these flags;" to which Sergeant Planciancois replied: "Colonel, I will bring these colors to you in honor, or report to God the reason why!" He fell, mortally wounded, in one of the many desperate charges at Port Hudson, with his face to the Enemy, and the colors in his hand.

Banks, in his Report, speaking of the Colored regiments, said: "Their conduct was heroic. No troops could be more determined or more daring. They made, during the day, three charges upon the batteries of the Enemy, suffering very heavy losses, and holding their positions at nightfall with the other troops on the right of our line. The highest commendation is bestowed upon them by all the officers in command on the right."

The New York Times' correspondent said:—"The deeds of heroism performed by these Colored men were such as the proudest White men might emulate. Their colors are torn to pieces by shot, and literally bespattered by blood and brains. The color-sergeant of the 1st Louisiana, on being mortally wounded (the top of his head taken off by a sixpounder), hugged the colors to his breast, when a struggle ensued between the two color-corporals on each side of him, as to who should have the honor of bearing the sacred standard, and during this generous contention one was seriously wounded."

So again, on Sunday the 6th of June following, at Milliken's Bend, where an African brigade, with 160 men of the 23rd Iowa, although surprised in camp by a largely superior force of the Enemy, repulsed him gallantly—of which action General Grant, in his official Report, said: "In this battle, most of the troops engaged were Africans, who had but little experience in the use of fire-arms. Their conduct is said, however, to have been most gallant."

So, also, in the bloody assault of July 18th, on Fort Wagner, which was led by the 54th Massachusetts (Colored) Regiment with intrepidity, and where they planted, and for some time maintained, their Country's flag on the parapet, until they "melted away before the Enemy's fire, their bodies falling down the slope and into the ditch."

And from that time on, through the War—at Wilson's Wharf, in the many bloody charges at Petersburg, at Deep Bottom, at Chapin's Farm, Fair Oaks, and numerous other battle-fields, in Virginia and elsewhere, right down to Appomattox—the African soldier fought courageously, fully vindicating the War-wisdom of Abraham Lincoln in emancipating and arming the Race.

The promulgation of this New Year's Proclamation of Freedom unquestionably had a wonderful effect in various ways, upon the outcome of the War.

It cleared away the cobwebs which the arguments of the loyal Border-State men, and of the Northern Copperheads and other Disunion and Pro-Slavery allies of the Rebels were forever weaving for the discouragement, perplexity and ensnarement, of the thoroughly loyal out-and-out Union men of the Land. It largely increased our strength in fighting material. It brought to us the moral support of the World, with the active sympathy of philanthropy's various forces. And besides, it correspondingly weakened the Rebels. Every man thus freed from his Bondage, and mustered into the Union Armies, was not only a gain of one man on the Union side, but a loss of one man to the Enemy. It is not, therefore, surprising that the Disunion Conspirators—whether at the South or at the North—were furious.

The Chief Conspirator, Jefferson Davis, had already, (December 23, 1862,) issued a proclamation of outlawry against General B. F. Butler, for arming certain Slaves that had become Free upon entering his lines—the two last clauses of which provided: "That all Negro Slaves captured in arms, be at once delivered over to the Executive authorities of the respective States to which they belong, to be dealt with according to the laws of said States," and "That the like orders be executed in all cases with respect to all commissioned Officers of the United States, when found serving in company with said Slaves in insurrection against the authorities of the different States of this Confederacy."

He now called the attention of the Rebel Congress to President Lincoln's two Proclamations of Emancipation, early in January of 1863; and that Body responded by adopting, on the 1st of May of that year, a Resolution, the character of which was so cold-bloodedly atrocious, that modern Civilization might well wonder and Christianity shudder at its purport. [It was in these words:

"Resolved, by the Congress of the Confederate States of America, In response to the Message of the President, transmitted to Congress at the commencement of the present session, That, in the opinion of Congress, the commissioned officers of the Enemy ought not to be delivered to the authorities of the respective States, as suggested in the said Message, but all captives taken by the Confederate forces ought to be dealt with and disposed of by the Confederate Government.

"SEC. 2.—That, in the judgment of Congress, the proclamations of the President of the United States, dated respectively September 22, 1862, and January 1, 1863, and the other measures of the Government of the United States and of its authorities, commanders, and forces, designed or tending to emancipate slaves in the Confederate States, or to abduct such slaves, or to incite them to insurrection, or to employ negroes in war against the Confederate States, or to overthrow the institution of African Slavery, and bring on a servile war in these States, would, if successful, produce atrocious consequences, and they are inconsistent with the spirit of those usages which, in modern warfare, prevail among civilized nations; they may, therefore, be properly and lawfully repressed by retaliation.

"SEC. 3.—That in every case wherein, during the present war, any violation of the laws or usages of war among civilized nations shall be, or has been, done and perpetrated by those acting under authority of the Government of the United States, on persons or property of citizens of the Confederate States, or of those under the protection or in the land or naval service of the Confederate States, or of any State of the Confederacy, the President of the Confederate States is hereby authorized to cause full and ample retaliation to be made for every such violation, in such manner and to such extent as he may think proper.

"SEC. 4.—That every white person, being a commissioned officer, or acting as such, who, during the present war, shall command negroes or mulattoes in arms against the Confederate States, or who shall arm, train, organize, or prepare negroes or mulattoes for military service against the Confederate States, or who shall voluntarily aid negroes or mulattoes in any military enterprise, attack, or conflict in such service, shall be deemed as inciting servile insurrection, and shall, if captured, be put to death, or be otherwise punished at the discretion of the Court.

"SEC. 5.—Every person, being a commissioned officer, or acting as such in the service of the Enemy, who shall, during the present war, excite, attempt to excite, or cause to be excited, a servile insurrection, or who shall incite, or cause to be incited, a slave to rebel, shall, if captured, be put to death, or be otherwise punished at the discretion of the court.

"SEC. 6.—Every person charged with an offense punishable under the preceding resolutions shall, during the present war, be tried before the military court attached to the army or corps by the troops of which he shall have been captured, or by such other military court as the President may direct, and in such manner and under such regulations as the President shall prescribe; and, after conviction, the President may commute the punishment in such manner and on such terms as he may deem proper.

"SEC. 7.—All negroes and mulattoes who shall be engaged in war, or be taken in arms against the Confederate States, or shall give aid or comfort to the enemies of the Confederate States, shall, when captured in the Confederate States, be delivered to the authorities of the State or States in which they shall be captured, to be dealt with according to the present or future laws of such State or States."]

But atrocious as were the provisions of the Resolution, or Act aforesaid, in that they threatened death or Slavery to every Black man taken with Union arms in his hand, and death to every White commissioned officer commanding Black soldiers, yet the manner in which they were executed was still more barbarous.

At last it became necessary to adopt some measure by which captured Colored Union soldiers might be protected equally with captured White Union soldiers from the frequent Rebel violations of the Laws of War in the cases of the former.

President Lincoln, therefore, issued an Executive Order prescribing retaliatory measures.

[In the following words:

"EXECUTIVE MANSION,

"WASHINGTON, July 30, 1863.

"It is the duty of every Government to give protection to its citizens, of whatever class, color, or condition, and especially to those who are duly organized as soldiers in the public service. The Law of Nations, and the usages and customs of War, as carried on by civilized Powers, permit no distinction as to color in the treatment of prisoners of War, as public enemies.

"To sell or Enslave any captured person, on account of his Color, and for no offense against the Laws of War, is a relapse into barbarism, and a crime against the civilization of the age.

"The Government of the United States will give the same protection to all its soldiers, and if the Enemy shall sell or Enslave any one because of his color, the offense shall be punished by Retaliation upon the Enemy's prisoners in our possession.

"It is therefore Ordered, that, for every soldier of the United States killed in violation of the Laws of War, a Rebel soldier shall be executed; and for every one Enslaved by the Enemy or sold into Slavery, a Rebel soldier shall be placed at hard work on the public works, and continued at such labor until the other shall be released and receive the treatment due to a prisoner of War.

"By order of the Secretary of War.

ABRAHAM LINCOLN. E. D.

TOWNSEND, Assistant Adjutant-General."]

It was hoped that the mere announcement of the decision of our Government to retaliate, would put an instant stop to the barbarous conduct of the Rebels toward the captured Colored Union troops, but the hope was vain. The atrocities continued, and their climax was capped by the cold-blooded massacres perpetrated by Forrest's 5,000 Cavalry, after capturing Fort Pillow, a short distance above Memphis, on the Mississippi river.

The garrison of that Fort comprised less than 600 Union soldiers, about one-half of whom were White, and the balance Black. These brave fellows gallantly defended the Fort against eight times their number, from before sunrise until the afternoon, when—having failed to win by fair means, under the Laws of War,—the Enemy treacherously crept up the ravines on either side of the Fort, under cover of flags of truce, and then, with a sudden rush, carried it, butchering both Blacks and Whites —who had thrown away their arms, and were striving to escape—until night temporarily put an end to the sanguinary tragedy.

On the following morning the massacre was completed by the butchery and torture of wounded remnants of these brave Union defenders—some being buried alive, and others nailed to boards, and burned to death.

[For full account of these hideous atrocities, see testimony of survivors before the Committee on Conduct and Expenditures of the War. (H. R. Report, No. 65, 1st S. 38th Cong.)]

And all this murderous malignity, for what?—Simply, and only, because one-half of the Patriot victims had Black skins, while the other half had dared to fight by the side of the Blacks!

In the after-days of the War, the cry with which our Union Black regiments went into battle:—"Remember Fort Pillow!"—inspired them to deeds of valor, and struck with terror the hearts of the Enemy. On many a bloody field, Fort Pillow was avenged.

It is a common error to suppose that the first arming of the Black man was on the Union side. The first Black volunteer company was a Rebel one, raised early in May, 1861, in the city of Memphis, Tenn.; and at Charleston, S. C., Lynchburg, Va., and Norfolk, Va., large bodies of Free Negroes volunteered, and were engaged, earlier than that, to do work on the Rebel batteries.

On June 28th of the same year, the Rebel Legislature of Tennessee passed an Act not only authorizing the Governor "to receive into the Military service of the State all male Free persons of Color between the ages of fifteen and fifty, or such number as may be necessary, who may be sound in mind and body, and capable of actual service," but also prescribing "That in the event a sufficient number of Free persons of Color to meet the wants of the State shall not tender their services, the Governor is empowered, through the Sheriffs of the different counties, to press such persons until the requisite number is obtained."

At a review of Rebel troops, at New Orleans, November 23, 1861, "One regiment comprised 1,400 Free Colored men." Vast numbers of both Free Negroes and Slaves were employed to construct Rebel fortifications throughout the War, in all the Rebel States. And on the 17th of February, 1864, the Rebel Congress passed an Act which provides in its first section "That all male Free Negroes * * * resident in the Confederate States, between the ages of eighteen and fifty years, shall be held liable to perform such duties with the Army, or in connection with the Military defenses of the Country, in the way of work upon the fortifications, or in Government works for the production or preparation of materials of War, or in Military hospitals, as the Secretary of War or the Commanding General of the Trans-Mississippi Department may, from time to time, prescribe:" while the third section provides that when the Secretary of War shall "be unable to procure the service of Slaves in any Military Department, then he is authorized to impress the services of as many male Slaves, not to exceed twenty thousand, as may be required, from time to time, to discharge the duties indicated in the first section of the Act."

And this Act of, the Rebel Congress was passed only forty days before the fiendish massacre of the Union Whites and Blacks who together, at Fort Pillow, were performing for the Union, "such duties with the Army," and "in connection with the Military defenses of the Country," as had been prescribed for them by their Commanding General!

Under any circumstances—and especially under this state of facts—nothing could excuse or palliate that shocking and disgraceful and barbarous crime against humanity; and the human mind is incapable of understanding how such savagery can be accounted for, except upon the theory that "He that nameth Rebellion nameth not a singular, or one only sin, as is theft, robbery, murder, and such like; but he nameth the whole puddle and sink of all sins against God and man; against his country, his countrymen, his children, his kinsfolk, his friends, and against all men universally; all sins against God and all men heaped together, nameth he that nameth Rebellion."

The inconsistency of the Rebels, in getting insanely and murderously furious over the arming of Negroes for the defense of the imperiled Union and the newly gained liberties of the Black Race, when they had themselves already armed some of them and made them fight to uphold the Slave-holders' Rebellion and the continued Enslavement of their race, is already plain enough.

[The writer is indebted to the courtesy of a prominent South Carolinian, for calling his attention to the "Singular coincidence, that a South Carolinian should have proposed in 1778, what was executed in 1863-64—the arming of Negroes for achieving their Freedom"—as shown in the following very curious and interesting letters written by the brave and gifted Colonel John Laurens, of Washington's staff, to his distinguished father:

HEAD QUARTERS, 14th Jan., 1778.

I barely hinted to you, my dearest father, my desire to augment the Continental forces from an untried source. I wish I had any foundation to ask for an extraordinary addition to those favours which I have already received from you. I would solicit you to cede me a number of your able bodied men slaves, instead of leaving me a fortune.

I would bring about a two-fold good; first I would advance those who are unjustly deprived of the rights of mankind to a state which would be a proper gradation between abject slavery and perfect liberty, and besides I would reinforce the defenders of liberty with a number of gallant soldiers. Men, who have the habit of subordination almost indelibly impressed on them, would have one very essential qualification of soldiers. I am persuaded that if I could obtain authority for the purpose, I would have a corps of such men trained, uniformly clad, equip'd and ready in every respect to act at the opening of the next campaign. The ridicule that may be thrown on the color, I despise, because I am sure of rendering essential service to my country.

I am tired of the languor with which so sacred a war as this is carried on. My circumstances prevent me from writing so long a letter as I expected and wish'd to have done on a subject which I have much at heart. I entreat you to give a favourable answer to

Your most affectionate

JOHN LAURENS.

The Honble Henry Laurens Esq.

President of Congress.

HEAD QUARTERS, 2nd Feb., 1778.

My Dear Father:

The more I reflect upon the difficulties and delays which are likely to attend the completing our Continental regiments, the more anxiously is my mind bent upon the scheme, which I lately communicated to you. The obstacles to the execution of it had presented themselves to me, but by no means appeared insurmountable. I was aware of having that monstrous popular prejudice, open-mouthed against me, of undertaking to transform beings almost irrational, into well disciplined soldiers, of being obliged to combat the arguments, and perhaps the intrigues, of interested persons. But zeal for the public service, and an ardent desire to assert the rights of humanity, determined me to engage in this arduous business, with the sanction of your consent. My own perseverance, aided by the countenance of a few virtuous men, will, I hope, enable me to accomplish it.

You seem to think, my dear father, that men reconciled by long habit to the miseries of their condition, would prefer their ignominious bonds to the untasted sweets of liberty, especially when offer'd upon the terms which I propose.

I confess, indeed, that the minds of this unhappy species must be debased by a servitude, from which they can hope for no relief but death, and that every motive to action but fear, must be nearly extinguished in them. But do you think they are so perfectly moulded to their state as to be insensible that a better exists? Will the galling comparison between themselves and their masters leave them unenlightened in this respect? Can their self love be so totally annihilated as not frequently to induce ardent wishes for a change?

You will accuse me, perhaps, my dearest friend, of consulting my own feelings too much; but I am tempted to believe that this trampled people have so much human left in them, as to be capable of aspiring to the rights of men by noble exertions, if some friend to mankind would point the road, and give them a prospect of success. If I am mistaken in this, I would avail myself, even of their weakness, and, conquering one fear by another, produce equal good to the public. You will ask in this view, how do you consult the benefit of the slaves? I answer, that like other men, they are creatures of habit. Their cowardly ideas will be gradually effaced, and they will be modified anew. Their being rescued from a state of perpetual humiliation, and being advanced as it were, in the scale of being, will compensate the dangers incident to their new state.

The hope that will spring in each man's mind, respecting his own escape, will prevent his being miserable. Those who fall in battle will not lose much; those who survive will obtain their reward. Habits of subordination, patience under fatigues, sufferings and privations of every kind, are soldierly qualifications, which these men possess in an eminent degree.

Upon the whole, my dearest friend and father, I hope that my plan for serving my country and the oppressed negro race will not appear to you the chimera of a young mind, deceived by a false appearance of moral beauty, but a laudable sacrifice of private interest, to justice and the public good.

You say, that my resources would be small, on account of the proportion of women and children. I do not know whether I am right, for I speak from impulse, and have not reasoned upon the matter. I say, altho' my plan is at once to give freedom to the negroes, and gain soldiers to the states; in case of concurrence, I should sacrifice the former interest, and therefore we change the women and children for able-bodied men. The more of these I could obtain, the better; but forty might be a good foundation to begin upon.

It is a pity that some such plan as I propose could not be more extensively executed by public authority. A well-chosen body of 5,000 black men, properly officer'd, to act as light troops, in addition to our present establishment, might give us decisive success in the next campaign.

I have long deplored the wretched state of these men, and considered in their history, the bloody wars excited in Africa, to furnish America with slaves—the groans of despairing multitudes, toiling for the luxuries of merciless tyrants.

I have had the pleasure of conversing with you, sometimes, upon the means of restoring them to their rights. When can it be better done, than when their enfranchisement may be made conducive to the public good, and be modified, as not to overpower their weak minds?

You ask, what is the general's opinion, upon this subject? He is convinced, that the numerous tribes of blacks in the southern parts of the continent, offer a resource to us that should not be neglected. With respect to my particular plan, he only objects to it, with the arguments of pity for a man who would be less rich than he might be.

I am obliged, my dearest friend and father, to take my leave for the present; you will excuse whatever exceptionable may have escaped in the course of my letter, and accept the assurance of filial love, and respect of

Your

JOHN LAURENS]

If, however, it be objected that the arming of Negroes by the Rebels was exceptional and local, and, that otherwise, the Rebels always used their volunteer or impressed Negro forces in work upon fortifications and other unarmed Military Works, and never proposed using them in the clash of arms, as armed soldiers against armed White men, the contrary is easily proven.

In a message to the Rebel Congress, November 7, 1864, Jefferson Davis himself, while dissenting at that time from the policy, advanced by many, of "a general levy and arming of the Slaves, for the duty of soldiers," none the less declared that "should the alternative ever be presented of subjugation, or of the employment of the Slave as a soldier, there seems no reason to doubt what should then be our decision."

In the meantime, however, he recommended the employment of forty thousand Slaves as pioneer and engineer laborers, on the ground that "even this limited number, by their preparatory training in intermediate duties Would form a more valuable reserve force in case of urgency, than threefold their number suddenly called from field labor; while a fresh levy could, to a certain extent, supply their places in the special service" of pioneer and engineer work; and he undertook to justify the inconsistency between his present recommendation, and his past attitude, by declaring that "A broad, moral distinction exists between the use of Slaves as soldiers in defense of their homes, and the incitement of the same persons to insurrection against their masters, for," said he, "the one is justifiable, if necessary; the other is iniquitous and unworthy of a civilized people."

So also, while a Bill for the arming of Slaves was pending before the Rebel Congress early in 1865, General Robert E. Lee wrote, February 18th, from the Headquarters of the Rebel Armies, to Hon. E. Barksdale, of the Rebel House of Representatives, a communication, in which, after acknowledging the receipt of a letter from him of February 12th, "with reference to the employment of Negroes as soldiers," he said: "I think the Measure not only expedient but necessary * * * in my opinion, the Negroes, under proper circumstances, will make efficient soldiers. * * * I think those who are employed, should be freed. It would be neither just nor wise, in my opinion, to require them to remain as Slaves"—thus, not only approving the employment of Black Slaves as soldiers, to fight White Union men, but justifying their Emancipation as a reward for Military service. And, a few days afterward, that Rebel Congress passed a Bill authorizing Jefferson Davis to take into the Rebel Army as many Negro Slaves "as he may deem expedient, for and during the War, to perform Military service in whatever capacity he may direct," and at the same time authorizing General Lee to organize them as other "troops" are organized.

[This Negro soldier Bill, according to McPherson's Appendix, p. 611-612, passed both Houses, and was in these words:

A Bill to increase the Military Forces of the Confederate States.

"The Congress of the Confederate States of America do Enact, That in order to provide additional forces to repel invasion, maintain the rightful possession of the Confederate States, secure their Independence and preserve their Institutions, the President be and he is hereby authorized to ask for and accept from the owners of Slaves the services of such number of able-bodied Negro men as he may deem expedient for and during the War, to perform Military service in whatever capacity he may direct.

"SEC. 2.—That the General-in-Chief be authorized to organize the said Slaves into companies, battalions, regiments, and brigades, under such rules and regulations as the Secretary of War may prescribe, and to be commanded by such officers as the President may appoint.

"SEC. 3.—That, while employed in the Service, the said troops shall receive the same rations, clothing, and compensation as are allowed to other troops in the same branch of the Service.

"SEC. 4.—That if, under the previous sections of this Act, the President shall not be able to raise a sufficient number of troops to prosecute the War successfully and maintain the Sovereignty of the States, and the Independence of the Confederate States, then he is hereby authorized to call on each State, whenever he thinks it expedient, for her quota of 300,000 troops, in addition to those subject to Military service, under existing laws, or so many thereof as the President may deem necessary, to be raised from such classes of the population, irrespective of color, in each State, as the proper authorities thereof may determine: Provided, that not more than 25 per cent. of the male Slaves, between the ages of 18 and 45, in any State, shall be called for under the provisions of this Act.

"SEC. 5.—That nothing in this Act shall be construed to authorize a change in the relation of said Slaves."]